NEW OXFORD ENGLISH

2

Anne Powling

John O'Connor

Geoff Barton

Oxford University Press

INTRODUCTION

New Oxford English has been devised to introduce you to every aspect of the new National Curriculum in English through enjoyable, stimulating activities and resources which are exciting and attractive to use. *Students' Books 1–3* are designed for use in Key Stage 3, or Years S1 and S2 in Scotland. *Students' Book 4* is aimed at students working towards GCSE and Standard Grade.

The four modules

Each book is divided into four sections, or 'modules', which reflect four major areas of work in the English classroom: Narrative, Poetry, Non-Fiction, and Drama.

- In the **Narrative** module you will learn about a range of narrative features, including how stories can be told through diary entries, how authors set the scene for a story, and what makes a good horror story.
- The **Poetry** module asks you to do everything from creating your own limericks to performing an extract from *Beowulf*, and offers a range of poems from writers as different as Lemn Sissay, Thomas Campbell, and Gillian Clarke.
- In **Non-Fiction** you will have the opportunity to examine a range of media from a variety of angles – including a look at how soft-drinks companies 'target' their markets, how local newspapers are put together, and how presentation affects what you think about written material.
- In the **Drama** module you will explore four of the main sources of inspiration for playwrights through the centuries – the myths of Ancient Greece, the Bible, history, and the imagination – and learn about the acting spaces in which their plays have been staged.

You can find full details of the range of extracts in *New Oxford English Book 2* on page 159 and see how it covers the National Curriculum Programmes of Study on page 3.

Language Study

After each module there is a Language Study unit, which deals with features of language work (such as grammar, punctuation or the development of the language) which have arisen from that particular module. For example, the Non-Fiction module contains extracts from 1930s magazines and this leads to work in the Language Study unit on what slang is and how it has changed through the ages.

Using New Oxford English

You are not expected to work in any set order through the modules in each book: you might be performing a play one day and discussing advertisements on the video the next. It is helpful, though, to link the features in the Language Study units with the modules to which they are attached. In that way, language work can arise naturally from the texts you are looking at or the activities you are engaged in.

Taking it further

These extension activities together with photocopiable sheets from the Teacher's Book will give you the opportunity to continue work you have particularly enjoyed and to develop your skills in English.

The video

A video accompanies each Students' Book and this permits you, for example, to see a poet at work in schools, think about advertisements, look inside the Globe Theatre, and take part in a newsroom simulation.

We hope that you will enjoy using and viewing New Oxford English.

New Oxford English 2 and the National Curriculum

PROGRAMMES OF STUDY	MODULE 1 NARRATIVE	MODULE 2 POETRY	MODULE 3 NON-FICTION	MODULE 4 DRAMA
Speaking and Listening				
1a Talking for different purposes	Telling Our Own Stories What Makes a Good Horror Story?	Limericks Reflecting on Pictures Rhythm in Poetry	Making News What Makes a Magazine? Image-making	The Murder of Agamemnon Writing about a 'Real' Setting
1b Talking in a range of contexts	Developing Character The Publishing Business	Opening Up • Shaping Poems • Sound Echoes Sense	Local News • Women's Magazines • Advertising	The Murder of Agamemnon The Thwarting of Baron Bolligrew
1c Listening attentively	That's What You Think What Makes a Good Horror Story?	Opening Up Another Box	Making News Women's Magazines	
1d Drama, role play, and performance	Developing Character The Publishing Business	Ballad • Rhythm in Poetry Sound Echoes Sense	Making News A New Magazine	The Murder of Agamemnon Judas and the Great Betrayal
2a Structuring and adapting talk	Telling Our Own Stories What Happened Next?	Rhythm in Poetry	Making News • A New Magazine • Image-making	Judas and the Great Betrayal
2b Effective listening and responding	A Room of Your Own The Publishing Business	Ballads Reflecting on Pictures	Making News	Changing the Audience
3a Using Standard English fluently and appropriately		Ballads Personification		
3b Development of the language		Where the English Language Came From	The Changing Language	Middle English
Reading				
1a Reading widely and independently	The Publishing Business	From Another Angle	Brochure or Travelogue? The Ends of the Earth	The Greek Theatre
1b Experiencing a variety of genres	A Life Exposed Developing Character What Happened Next?	Limericks Ballads Personification	Local News • Magazines The Coca-Cola Story Brochure or Travelogue?	Oedipus and the Circle of Fate Judas and the Mysteries Writing about a 'Real' Setting
1c Reading texts from different cultures	A Life Exposed	Rhythm in Poetry	The Ends of the Earth	Stories from Ancient Greece
1d Reading works from the literary heritage	The Scene of the Crime What Makes a Good Horror Story?	Ballads Alliteration		Judas and the Great Betrayal Writing about 'Real' People The Tempest • Middle English
1e Reading non-fiction texts	Telling Our Own Stories		Local News • Magazines Handwriting Styles The Ends of the Earth	Stories from Ancient Greece The Greek Theatre Shakespeare's Sources
1f Appreciating a range of media			Women's Magazines Advertising: Past and Present	Shakespeare's Theatre Red Dwarf
2a Reading for deeper meanings	Developing Character What Happened Next?	Opening Up • Reflecting on Pictures • From Another Angle	Women's Magazines Making Judgements	The Murder of Agamemnon Writing about a 'Real' Setting
2b Developing informed views on reading	That's What You Think Rural Landscape The Publishing Business	Another Box Ballads Personification	Local News Magazines: Past and Present The Coca-Cola Story	Judas and the Mysteries
2c Sifting and evaluating non-fiction texts	Telling Our Own Stories		Local News • Magazines Making Judgements	Shakespeare's Sources Shakespeare's Theatre
3a Recognizing features of different types of text	A Life Exposed • What Makes a Good Horror Story?	Ballads Rhythm in Poetry	Magazines: Past and Present Brochure or Travelogue?	Oedipus • Play Script, Dialogue and Reported Speech
3b Literary language and use of language in non-fiction	A Life Exposed Rural Landscape What Happened Next?	Opening Up • Reflecting on Pictures • Personification • Alliteration	Making News Magazines: Past and Present Making Judgements	Changing the Audience
Writing				
1a Developing written style	Telling Our Own Stories Developing Character The Publishing Business	Ballads • Onomatopoeia Alliteration • Synonyms	Making News Magazines: Past and Present The Ends of the Earth	Writing about a 'Real' Setting
1b Writing for different purposes and audiences	Developing Character The Publishing Business	Limericks Alliteration	Making News Magazines: Past and Present	Changing the Audience Shakespeare's Theatre
1c Writing in a variety of forms	Telling Our Own Stories That's What You Think The Publishing Business	Limericks Ballads Reflecting on Pictures	Making News The Ends of the Earth	Oedipus and the Circle of Fate Shakespeare's Theatre The Tempest
2a Planning, drafting, and presentation	Rural Landscape A Room of Your Own	Another Box • From Another Angle • Shaping Poems	Making News Making Judgements	Changing the Audience Red Dwarf
2b Displaying knowledge of text features in own writing	A Life Exposed That's What You Think Rural Landscape	Limericks • Ballads Reflecting on Pictures Verse Pictures	Magazines: Past and Present Brochure or Travelogue?	Oedipus and the Circle of Fate Play Script, Dialogue and Reported Speech
2c Increasing spelling knowledge	Nouns	Rhythm in Poetry Onomatopoeia	Image-making	Prefixes
2d Using neat, legible handwriting		Shaping Poems	Making Judgements Image-making	Oedipus and the Circle of Fate
3a Writing in Standard English and developing knowledge of register	Telling Our Own Stories Writing in Non-Standard English	Ballads	Making News Magazines: Past and Present Making Judgements	The Tempest
3b Understanding sentence level grammar and whole text organisation	Direct and Reported Speech Nouns	Verbs of Doing and Being	Using Adjectives More about Adverbs Looking at Sentences	Play Script, Dialogue and Reported Speech
3c Using reference texts for extending vocabulary		Limericks • Shaping Poems Alliteration • Synonyms		Prefixes

CONTENTS

MODULE 1 NARRATIVE

Diaries and Journals

Setting the Scene

Horror!

Language Study

MODULE 2 POETRY

Poem as Story

Poem as Picture

Poem as Shape

Poem as Sound

Language Study

CONTENTS

Diaries and Journals

Telling our own Stories: Zlata's Diary

The diary below was kept by a twelve-year-old girl before and during the conflict in Sarajevo. She uses it to try and understand the terrible events she is witnessing, to record what happens, and, at times, to pour out her anger and frustration. Reading it, we can begin to get a picture of what war means to the lives of ordinary people caught up in the conflict.

Thinking it through

Below are printed seven entries spread over an eighteen-month period. Listen to the entries read aloud and with a partner list all the ways Zlata's life has been changed.

Zlata's Diary

Wednesday, 27 May 1992

Dear Mimmy,

SLAUGHTER! MASSACRE! HORROR! CRIME! BLOOD! SCREAMS! TEARS! DESPAIR!

That's what Vaso Miskin Street looks like today. Two shells exploded in the street and one in the market. Mummy was nearby at the time. She ran to Grandma's and Grandad's. Daddy and I were beside ourselves because she hadn't come home. I saw some of it on TV but I still can't believe what I actually saw. It's unbelievable. I've got a lump in my throat and a knot in my tummy. HORRIBLE. They're taking the wounded to the hospital. It's a madhouse. We kept going to the window hoping to see Mummy, but she wasn't back. They released a list of the dead and wounded. Daddy and I were tearing our hair out. We didn't know what had happened to her. Was she alive? At 16.00, Daddy decided to go and check the hospital. He got dressed, and I got ready to go to the Bobars', so as not to stay at home alone. I looked out the window one more time and ... I SAW MUMMY RUNNING ACROSS THE BRIDGE. As she came into the house she started shaking and crying. Through her tears she told us how she had seen dismembered bodies. All the neighbours came because they had been afraid for her. Thank God, Mummy is with us. Thank God.

A HORRIBLE DAY. UNFORGETTABLE. HORRIBLE! HORRIBLE!

Your Zlata

Wednesday, 27 May 1992 Bosnian gunmen view the carnage on the street, after mortar shells landed amid a crowd of people waiting to buy bread in central Sarajevo. 20 people were reported killed, and dozens were injured in the incident, which happened as people were encouraged onto the streets by the relative quiet of a two-day ceasefire.

Sunday, 11 October 1992

Dear Mimmy,

Today is a day to be remembered in my family. Today we brought the wood-burning stove into the kitchen. It's nice and warm.

Mummy and Daddy and I all had a bath. It was rain water, but it doesn't matter. We're clean, and we didn't freeze, like the past few days.

There's still no electricity or water.

Your Zlata

Wednesday, 14 October 1992

Dear Mimmy,

I'm writing to you again by the light of one of my favourite candles. I lit it with a heavy heart. But we have to get light from somewhere.

Thursday, 25 February 1993

Auntie Ivanka received a package from Belgrade and brought me all sorts of things. Chocolate, ham (OOOH!), instant mashed potatoes, sugar, coffee, macaroni. Thank you, Auntie Ivanka! And Auntie Radmila brought me powdered milk. Imagine how everyone is thinking of me, a child hungry for everything. I got three letters from French children through a humanitarian organization. They were colourful New Year cards that arrived late. They were full of love and warm wishes for peace in Sarajevo. One of them came with coloured magic markers, which I used to draw them a heart.

Zlata

Tuesday, 18 August 1992

Dear Mimmy,

Mummy is carrying home the water. It's hard on her, but she has to do it. The water hasn't come back on. Nor has the electricity.

I didn't tell you, Mimmy, but I've forgotten what it's like to have water pouring out of a tap, what it's like to shower. We use a jug now. The jug has replaced the shower. We wash dishes and clothes like in the Middle Ages. This war is taking us back to olden times. And we take it, we suffer it, but we don't know for how long.

Zlata

Zlata Filipovic

Sunday, 5 September 1993

Dear Mimmy,

Today we heard that letters aren't coming into Sarajevo any more. There's something worse than not having electricity, water and gas, and that's not getting letters, which are our only contact with the outside world. Now we've lost that as well. It's just too much!

Žika brought me something wonderful today. A real live orange. Mummy said: 'Let's see whether I remember how to peel it.' And, and... she remembered. She did it. It was so nice and juicy. YUMMY!

Thursday, 7 October 1993

Dear Mimmy,

Things are the way they used to be, lately. There's no shooting (thank God), I go to school, read, play the piano...

Winter is approaching, but we have nothing to heat with.

I look at the calendar and it seems as though this year of 1993 will again be marked by war. God, we've lost two years listening to gunfire, battling with electricity, water, food, and waiting for peace.

I look at Mummy and Daddy. In two years they've aged ten. And me? I haven't aged, but I've grown, although I honestly don't know how. I don't eat fruit or vegetables, I don't drink juices, I don't eat meat... I am a child of rice, peas and spaghetti. There I am talking about food again. I often catch myself dreaming about chicken, a good cutlet, pizza, lasagne... Oh, enough of that.
Zlata

Zlata Filipovic

A parcel for Zlata

1 In your pair read back through the extracts and imagine you are packing an aid parcel for Zlata. You have a shoe box to fill. What does she enjoy and miss? What will you send her to help her? You will need to discuss what sort of person you think Zlata is.

2 In your pair, present the box to the class, explaining what you have packed and justifying your choice to the group.

3 In your box you are going to put a letter, since they are obviously very important to her. In your letter, explain:
- who you are and why you wanted to write
- why you have sent what you have
- what you have learned from the diary

Include any popular news you think may interest a twelve-year-old.

A Life Exposed

In the 1980s, the author Gary Paulsen decided to write a biography of a black American plantation slave called Sally Hemmings. She was owned by Thomas Jefferson, and during her time as his slave, she taught herself and her seven children to read and write.

While he was researching Sally Hemmings' life, the author discovered a great deal more about how slaves lived. He was inspired to write *Nightjohn*, a powerful story told through the eyes of one slave, a girl called Sarny.

In the extract below, Sarny watches as a new slave is brought into the compound.

A fictional diary

1 Read the extract through in a pair and note down all the detail you can on the following:
   - who you think Sarny, Waller, and Nightjohn are
   - how the slaves lived
   - how you feel about what you have just read

   What clues do you have about how Sarny feels about Waller and Nightjohn?

2 Share your findings as a class and discuss your feelings about what you have just read.

Nightjohn

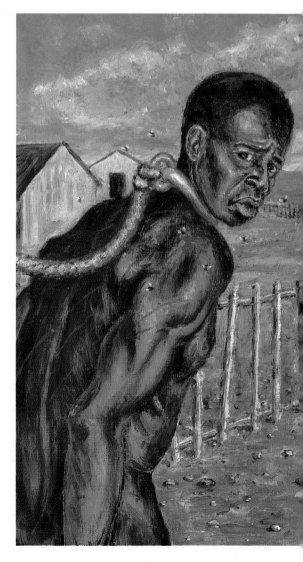

Old Waller brought him in bad.

Not in the wagon. He was walking, all alone in front of the horse. Waller riding the big brown horse in back. Had a rope down and over to a shackle on Nightjohn's neck. Rope tied to the saddle. So when the horse stopped, Nightjohn he stopped, jerked on his neck.

Nightjohn he didn't have any clothes on, stood naked in the sun. I was by the quarters, carrying water to wash the eating trough before it was time for the evening
10 feeding and I saw them.

Standing in the sun with the rope going from his neck up to the saddle, tired and sweating because Waller ran him. Dust all over him. Flies around his shoulders.

His back was all over scars from old whippings. The skin across his shoulders and down was raised in ripples, thick as my hand, up and down his back and onto his rear end and down his legs some.

In a little, Waller he untied the rope. Then he cracked the whip once or twice like he be a big man and drives
20 Nightjohn past the quarters and out to the field to work. Didn't matter that he'd been run or might be thirsty. He didn't stop at the pump but ran him right on through and out to the fields, naked as he was born, to get to hoeing.

Two times a day at the wooden trough – that's how we eat. Mornings they pour buttermilk down the trough and we dip cornbread in it and sometimes pieces of pork fat.

We take turns on a calabash gourd for a dipper to get all the milk out except the little ones don't always get much of a turn and have to lick the bottom of the trough when it's
30 done. For midday meal the field hands – men and women both, 'less a woman is a breeder in her last month, then she can work the yard – each carry a piece of cornbread and pork fat or meat with them. When the sun is high overhead they stop long enough to stand and eat the bread and fat. They don't get to sit or rest. Even do they have to do their business they dig a hole with their hoe and do it standing and cover it with dirt and get back to work.

Don't they do this, don't they do it right, don't they keep standing and work even to eat and do their business,
40 don't they do it all just exactly right the whip comes down on them. Old Waller he don't have overseers but they's two men he calls drivers. They have whips and clubs and use them.

Then at night, when it's just dark they come in from the fields. During the day mammy and the breeders that can still walk and the small ones that can't keep up to work in the fields yet make food.

We cook in the big pot mammy used for praying. We cook pork fat and vegetables from the garden and make
50 skillet cornbread. When the field people come in at night we pour from the pot in the trough and everybody passes the gourd and eats with their hands and dips cornbread into the juice till it's gone. Then the young ones get to lick the trough and we go into the quarters for the night.

Those to work in the field are always tired. Always caved in with work. And there ain't never enough to eat, so they be hungry, too. They usually go to sleep as soon as they hit the corn-shuck pallets on the floor.

Gary Paulsen

A slave's life

1 In your pair, try writing a short paragraph, suitable for an encyclopaedia, in which you describe a typical day in the life of a plantation slave. Include such detail as:
 ■ where they sleep
 ■ what they eat
 ■ what they are expected to do
 ■ particular hardships and problems

2 As a class, listen to some of these read aloud and discuss how they are different to the first account you read. What is lost in the second piece of writing? Why do you think the writer has chosen to tell the story through Sarny's eyes?

3 What is there about Sarny's character that makes her a good narrator?

Developing Character

The next extracts introduce us to another fictional character, Leigh Botts. His parents are separated, and he lives with his mum. Advised by author Mr Henshaw to keep a diary to help him with his own writing, Leigh reveals his changing feelings for his dad, a long-distance lorry driver, through his diary entries.

Reading and discussion

Divide yourselves into groups of four and take it in turns to share the following extracts. As you finish each one, take time to discuss the questions that follow.

Dear Mr Henshaw

Monday, December 25

Dear Mr Pretend Henshaw,

Last night I was feeling low and was still awake after the petrol station stopped pinging. Then I heard heavy feet coming up the steps, and for a minute I thought it was Dad until I remembered he always ran up steps.

Mom is careful about opening the door at night. I heard her turn on the outside light and knew she was peeking out from behind the curtain. She opened the door, and a man said, 'Is this where Leigh Botts lives?'

I was out of bed and into the front room in a second. 'I'm Leigh Botts,' I said.

'Your Dad asked me to drop this off for you.' A man who looked like a trucker handed me a big package.

'Thanks,' I said. 'Thanks a whole lot.' I must have looked puzzled because he said, 'He sent out a call over his CB radio for someone coming to Pacific Grove who would like to play Santa. So here I am. Merry Christmas and a ho-ho-ho!' He waved and was off down the walk before I could say anything more.

'Wow!' I said to Mom. 'Wow!' She just stood there in her robe smiling while I began to tear off the paper even if it wasn't Christmas morning. Dad had sent what I always wanted – a quilted down jacket with a lot of pockets and a hood that zips into the collar. I tried it on over my pyjamas. It was the right size and felt great. Getting a present from my Dad in time for Christmas felt even better.

The present

1 Why is Leigh so low at the start of this extract?
2 What does the last sentence tell us?
3 How does this entry make you feel about Mr Botts?

2

Sunday, February 4

Dear Mr Pretend Henshaw,

I hate my father.

All I wanted was to hear the phone ringing in Dad's trailer which wouldn't cost Mom anything because nobody would answer.

Except Dad answered. I almost hung up. He wasn't off in some other state. He was in his trailer, and he hadn't phoned me. 'You promised to phone me this week and you didn't,' I said. I felt I had to talk to him.

'Take it easy, kid,' he said. 'I just didn't get around to it. I was going to call this evening. The week isn't over yet.'

'I hoped you would call,' I said. 'I waited and waited.' Then I was sorry I said it. I have some pride left.

'There was heavy snow in the mountains,' he said. 'I had to chain up on Highway 80 and lost time.'

From my map book I know Highway 80 crosses the Sierra. I also know about putting chains on trucks. When the snow is heavy, truckers have to put chains on the drive wheels – all eight of them. Putting chains on eight big wheels in the snow is no fun. I felt a little better. 'How's Bandit?' I asked, as long as we were talking.

There was a funny silence. For a minute I thought the line was dead. Then I knew something must have happened to my dog.

'How's Bandit?' I asked again, louder in case Dad might have lost some of the hearing in his left ear from all that wind rushing by.

'Well, kid–' he began.

'My name is Leigh!' I almost yelled. 'I'm not just some kid you met on the street.'

'Keep your shirt on, Leigh,' he said. 'When I had to stop along with some other truckers to put on chains, I let Bandit out of the cab. I thought he would get right back in because it was snowing so hard, but after I chained up, he wasn't in the cab.'

'Did you leave the door open for him?' I asked.

Big pause. 'I could've sworn I did,' he said which meant he didn't. Then he said, 'I whistled and whistled, but Bandit didn't come. I couldn't wait any longer because the highway patrol was talking about closing Highway 80. I couldn't get stranded up there in the mountains when I had a deadline for delivering a load of TV sets to a dealer in Denver. I had to leave. I'm sorry, kid – Leigh – but that's the way it is.'

'You left Bandit to freeze to death.' I was crying from anger. How could he?

'Bandit knows how to take care of himself,' said Dad. 'I'll bet dollars to doughnuts he jumped into another truck that was leaving.'

I wiped my nose on my sleeve. 'Why would the driver let him?' I asked.

'Because he thought Bandit was lost,' said Dad, 'and he had to get on with his load before the highway was closed, the same as I did. He couldn't leave a dog to freeze.'

'What about your CB radio?' I asked. 'Didn't you send out a call?'

'Sure I did, but I didn't get an answer. Mountains cut down on reception,' Dad told me.

I was about to say I understood, but here comes the bad part, the really bad part. I heard a boy's voice say, 'Hey, Bill, Mom wants to know when we're going to get the pizza?' I felt as if my insides were falling out. I hung up. I didn't want to hear any more, when Mom had to pay for the phone call. I didn't want to hear any more at all.

'I hate my father'

1 What does Leigh mean by the sentence, 'I have some pride left'?

2 What has his father done to make Leigh hate him?

3 Do you think Leigh is right in his judgement?

Between events in this extract and the next, Leigh gets twenty dollars and a note from his dad, written on a napkin, apologizing roughly for what happened to Bandit. Leigh is furious.

For a while after that, Leigh does not hear from his dad. Then he gets a phone call.

3 ▸

Friday, March 26

It was Dad. My stomach felt as if it was dropping to the floor, the way it always does when I hear his voice. 'How're you doing, kid?' he asked.

His call took me so by surprise that I could feel my heart pounding, and I couldn't think of anything to say.

Then Dad surprised me. He asked, 'Do you ever miss your old Dad?'

I had to think for a minute. I missed him all right, but I couldn't seem to get the words out. My silence must have bothered him because he asked, 'Are you still there?'

'Sure, Dad, I miss you,' I told him. It was true, but not as true as it had been a couple of months ago. I still wanted him to pull up in front of the house in his big rig, but now I knew I couldn't count on it.

Leigh's reaction

1 Why does Leigh's stomach drop when he hears from his dad?

2 How are his feelings changing and why?

It is obvious from the previous extract that Leigh has learned a lot about his dad. The next extract is taken from a year later. As you read it, consider what more Leigh learns from the events that follow.

4

Saturday, March 31

Bandit came over to me, wagging his tail and looking happy. He was wearing a new red bandanna around his neck.

'How're you doing, kid?' asked Dad. 'I brought your dog back.'

'Gee, thanks,' I said, hugging Bandit. Dad's stomach hung over his belt, and he wasn't as tall as I remembered him.

'You've grown,' he said which is what grownups always say when they don't know what else to say to kids.

Did Dad expect me to stop growing just because he hadn't been around? 'How did you find Bandit?' I asked.

'By asking every day over my CB,' he said. 'I finally got an answer from a trucker who said he had picked up a lost dog in a snowstorm in the Sierra, a dog that was still riding with him. Last week we turned up in the same line at a weigh scale.'

'I'm sure glad you got him back,' I said, and after trying to think of something else to say, I asked, 'How come you're not hauling anything?' I think I hoped he would say he had driven all the way from Bakersfield just to bring Bandit back to me.

'I'm waiting for a reefer to be loaded with broccoli in Salinas,' he told me. 'Since it wasn't far, I thought I'd take a run over here before I take off for Ohio.'

So Dad had come to see me just because of broccoli. After all these months when I had longed to see him, it took a load of broccoli to get him here. I felt let down and my feelings hurt.

They hurt so much I couldn't think of anything to say. Dad looked tired and sad in a way I had never seen him look before.

Mom was taking such a long time making coffee I felt I had to entertain Dad so I showed him my Yearbook and what I had written. He read it and said, 'Funny, but I still think about that day every time I haul grapes to a winery. I'm glad you remember it, too.' That made me feel good. He looked at me awhile as if he expected to see... I don't know what. Then he rumpled my hair and said, 'You're smarter than your old man.'

That embarrassed me. I didn't know how to answer.

He stood up and so did I. Then he gave me a big hug, and for a minute I wanted to hang on to him and never let him go.

'So long, Leigh,' Dad said and started the motor. Then he leaned out and said, 'You're a good kid, Leigh. I'm proud of you, and I'll try not to let you down.' Then as he drove off, he yelled, 'See you around!' and sounded more the way I had remembered him.

Maybe it was broccoli that brought Dad to Salinas, but he had come the rest of the way because he really wanted to see us.

He had really missed us. I felt sad and a whole lot better at the same time.

Beverly Cleary

Father and son

1 'There are two sides to every argument.' How does this statement link to extract 4?

2 'I felt sad but a whole lot better at the same time.' How is it possible to feel both these things? Explain Leigh's feelings at the end of the last entry.

Charting a response

1 Using the ideas from your discussion, now try and chart Leigh's changing feelings on the graph below. Put an entry for each of Leigh's extracts and join your line up at the end.

2 Compare your chart with that of another group, explaining your points. How far did you agree?

Changing feelings

1 In your own words, explain how Leigh's feelings for his father change during the entries, and what you think he has learned by the end.

2 Write the diary for Leigh's father after his visit to the house. What has he learned over the past year and what does he think of his son? The following activities will help you to prepare for this.

■ In your original groups, prepare a set of questions that you would like to ask Mr Botts about his behaviour over the past year.

■ Exchange questions with another group and discuss your answers to their questions.

■ Your teacher will now choose one person from each group to be Mr Botts and collectively they will answer any questions the class can devise. Use this hot-seating to write Mr Botts' diary.

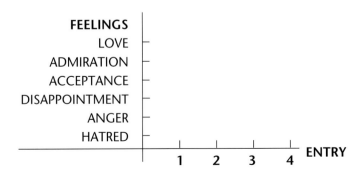

That's What You Think

In the extracts that follow, the diary of a fifteen-year-old has been put alongside that of her mother.

Contrasting points of view in diaries

In a pair, listen to the diaries read aloud and make a note of the differences in point of view between the two parties. What effect does this have on a reader?

Not Dressed Like That, You Don't!

13th December

Only one more week of school – seems impossible I've survived, but here I am. The school disco last night was FANTASTIC, once I got there. Nearly didn't make it – the parents tumbled that the skirt and T-shirt I had on was not what I was really going to wear. Mum spotted my bag. I had to show them the black stuff – thank God Sadie was looking after the belts and chains or I don't think they would have let me leave. As it was, there was a bit of fuss about me looking like a widow but then Mum acted like she was a real cool parent – said I didn't need to sneak out of the house and change somewhere else, I could have put the stuff on at home. If she could have seen me after we left Cathy's she would have laid an egg. Cathy lent me her make-up, and Sadie got our hair just right.

The old fogey at the door didn't want to let us in – he's somebody's parent. Almost makes mine look trendy. Half the teachers didn't recognize us, and half had a good laugh.

Sadie was in a bit of a huff because they thought we were dressing up for a joke, but I told her that to be misunderstood by the likes of them was actually a compliment – who wants to be on the same wavelength as people who watch 'World in Action' and nearly wet themselves if they miss the nine o'clock news? She cheered up after that.

The best bit of all was that David Slater was really knocked out by the gear – asked how long the make-up had taken, and whether we went for that look all the time. I said only on special occasions, and he laughed. He said that was good, because he'd been planning to ask if I wanted to go sailing over the holidays, but he couldn't cope with me looking like that on a boat! Then he asked me for a DANCE!!!!

To be truthful, it was not all that romantic. It was a disco number rather than a smoochy, and we didn't actually touch. But with the music so loud we had to get quite close to shout in each other's ear! I was very hopeful, but he had to leave early for some reason (he did tell me but I couldn't hear what he was saying properly). Still, at least he didn't dance with anyone else. I'm in with a chance, surely(?).

He's got to go to his grandparents for Christmas, too. I just knew we would have a lot in common. Anyway, he's going to give me a call after Christmas to fix up some sailing. IS THIS A DATE?!

I was late back from the disco – it took me ages to get that stuff out of my hair. Mum talked about 'responsibility' and 'concern for others' as usual, but who cares? David Slater had noticed me!

13th December

Jenny gave us a good laugh last night. It was the school disco, and she and Sadie have been whispering in corners about it for weeks. Mike and I couldn't figure out what they were up to, and I was beginning to get quite worried about what they had planned.

When it was time for her to leave, Jenny came downstairs wearing a very ordinary – suspiciously ordinary – skirt and T-shirt.

Clutched in her hand, half-hidden behind her back, was a bulging carrier bag. The way she edged towards the door, thinking she was being very cunning, was a hoot. I asked her what was in the bag and she went bright red.

'Just me boots,' she muttered. 'In case it rains.' Honestly, I could have fallen off my chair, but I kept a straight face and asked to see. Jenny's expression turned sour, and she half threw me the bag. Inside were some awful black rags (skirt, top and old man's waistcoat, by the look of it) and some lengths of tatty black lace. Underneath it all were the Doc Marten's we bought her for last year's walking holiday.

She was obviously intending to change somewhere else – Catherine's house would be my bet – and transform herself into one of those hideous Gothic creatures. Presumably Sadie or Catherine had the make-up and hair glue waiting. And here was I thinking all sorts of things – I even thought she might be planning to take drink or drugs. School discos in my day were dreadful for that sort of thing.

To find out it was just a costume was quite a relief. Not that I told that to Jenny, of course. I acted surprised, and said if it was only black clothes she was trying to hide, it wasn't worth the bother. We don't mind what she wears, after all.

Jenny went off with a smug smile, thinking she had pulled one over on us, and Mike and I settled down to a quiet evening without her stereo blasting through the place. A good time had by all, I should say.

I think Jenny forgot about the time it would take to restore herself to 'normal' because she was half an hour late back, and even then she looked like a battered panda. I bet she must have been a sight in the full regalia. I wish I could have seen it. Anyway, I gave her the usual lecture about being late, but it was hard not to laugh.

Yvonne Coppard

Discussing the issues

As a class, discuss and list the things that are most likely to spark off arguments between you and your parents.

Writing another entry

Now write David Slater's diary entry for the evening. You may want to include some of the following:

1 Was David hoping Jenny would be there?
2 What did he think of her clothes?
3 Why did he have to leave early – what was the real reason?
4 Is he considering asking her out?

Taking it further

The characters of Jenny and her parents could be developed through a series of diary entries. These could focus on the sort of events you discussed earlier, where you and your parents are most likely to fall out. For instance, what might happen if Jenny threw a party and her parents insisted on being there?

Setting the Scene

In this unit, you'll be asked to consider the settings that authors use for their stories. For each setting try to think about:

- the kind of atmosphere that is created
- how the characters react to this atmosphere
- how the author creates this atmosphere

The Scene of the Crime

Looking at settings

In a pair, listen to the extracts below being read aloud to you, then see if you can decide:

- where the action is happening
- what has taken place
- how the watchers feel about events

Fireweed

The eastern sky, as in a monstrous sunrise, was an expanse of limpid golden light, as though the sky itself was a wall of fire. Against it we could see the slender spires of Wren's churches, and the great dome of St Paul's. They were not quite mere silhouettes; the corners, the columns, the curve of the dome had been traced in lines of reflected light, as though they had been drawn with a pencil of flame. London was burning. It was all on fire. The immensity of it quenched my own fear in a wave of awe; it seemed like the end of the world.

Our danger was only, after all, a small thing, seen in that light. I got right up, stood up, and pulled her to her feet too. Leading her by the hand I went on over the bridge, walking steadily. At the other end of the bridge was a little hut, a fire-watcher's post. In front of it a man was sitting, on a pile of sandbags. Round his neck hung a pair of binoculars, and a field telephone dangled in his drooped hand. His head was thrown back, so that the light of the burning city drew a circle of gold round his face, on the under side of the rim of his helmet. As we passed him I saw that his eyes were open, and the fire glinted in them too. They were still shining, still moist; he was very newly dead.

Jill Paton Walsh

Treasure Island

Indeed, as we found when we also reached the spot, it was something very different. At the foot of a pretty big pine, and involved in a green creeper, which had even partly lifted some of the smaller bones, a human skeleton lay, with a few shreds of clothing, on the ground. I believe a chill struck for a moment to every heart.

'He was a seaman,' said George Merry, who, bolder than the rest, had gone up close, and was examining the rags of clothing. 'Leastways, this is good sea-cloth.'

'Ay, ay,' said Silver, 'like enough; you wouldn't look to find a bishop here, I reckon. But what sort of a way is that for bones to lie? 'Tain't in natur'.'

Indeed, on a second glance, it seemed impossible to fancy that the body was in a natural position. But for some disarray (the work, perhaps, of the birds that had fed upon him, or of the slow-growing creeper that had gradually enveloped his remains) the man lay perfectly straight – his feet pointing in one direction, his hands, raised above his head like a diver's, pointing directly in the opposite.

'I've taken a notion into my old numskull,' observed Silver. 'Here's the compass; there's the tip-top p'int o' Skeleton Island, stickin' out like a tooth. Just take a bearing, will you, along the line of them bones.'

It was done. The body pointed straight in the direction of the island, and the compass read duly ESE. and by E.

'I thought so,' cried the cook; 'this here is a p'inter. Right up there is our line for the Pole Star and the jolly dollars. But, by thunder! if it don't make me cold inside to think of Flint. This is one of *his* jokes, and no mistake. Him and these six was alone here; he killed 'em, every man; and this one he hauled here and laid down by compass, shiver my timbers! They're long bones, and the hair's been yellow. Ay, that would be Allardyce. You mind Allardyce, Tom Morgan?'

'Ay, ay,' returned Morgan, 'I mind him; he owed me money, he did, and took my knife ashore with him.'

'Speaking of knives,' said another, 'why don't we find his'n lying round? Flint warn't the man to pick a seaman's pocket; and the birds, I guess, would leave it be.'

'By the powers, and that's true!' cried Silver.

'There ain't a thing left here,' said Merry, still feeling round among the bones, 'not a copper doit nor a baccy box. It don't look nat'ral to me.'

'No, by gum, it don't,' agreed Silver; 'not nat'ral, nor not nice, says you. Great guns! messmates, but if Flint was living, this would be a hot spot for you and me. Six they were, and six are we; and bones is what they are now.'

'I saw him dead with these here deadlights,' said Morgan. 'Billy took me in. There he laid, with penny-pieces on his eyes.'

'Dead – ay, sure enough he's dead and gone below,' said the fellow with the bandage; 'but if ever sperrit walked, it would be Flint's. Dear heart, but he died bad, did Flint!'

'Ay, that he did,' observed another; 'now he raged, and now he hollered for the rum, and now he sang. "Fifteen Men" were his only song, mates; and I tell you true, I never rightly liked to hear it since. It was main hot, and the windy was open, and I hear that old song comin' out as clear as clear – and the death-haul on the man already.'

'Come, come,' said Silver, 'stow this talk. He's dead, and he don't walk, that I know; leastways, he won't walk by day, and you may lay to that. Care killed a cat. Fetch ahead for the doubloons.'

We started, certainly; but in spite of the hot sun and the staring daylight, the pirates no longer ran separate and shouting through the wood, but kept side by side and spoke with bated breath. The terror of the dead buccaneer had fallen on their spirits.

Robert Louis Stevenson

Characters' reactions

Both passages deal with death and how the characters react to what they see.

1 What are the differences between the reactions of the pair in the first extract and the reaction of the pirates in the second?

2 What atmosphere is created in each passage?

Make a note of the lines or phrases that gave you the clues for your answers.

Compare your findings with the rest of the class.

Rural Landscape

Under Milk Wood

The sunny slow lulling afternoon yawns and — through the dozy town.
The sea lolls, laps and — in, with fishes — in its lap. The meadows still
as Sunday, the shut-eye tasselled bulls, the goat-and-daisy dingles, —
happy and lazy. The dumb duck-ponds snooze. Clouds — and pillow
on Llaregyb Hill. Pigs grunt in a wet wallow-bath, and smile as they —
and dream. They dream of the acorned swill of the world, the rooting
for pig-fruit, the bag-pipe dugs of the mother sow, the squeal and
snuffle of yesses of the women pigs in rut. They — and snout in the
pig-loving sun; their tails curl; they rollick and slobber and — to deep,
smug, after-swill sleep. Donkeys angelically — on Donkey Down.

Dylan Thomas

Creating an atmosphere

1 In a pair, try to find two or three
   adjectives to describe the atmosphere
   created in Dylan Thomas' piece.
2 It is the author's choice of words that
   helps to convey the atmosphere created.
   - With a partner, try to find your own
     words to fill the gaps left in the piece.
   - Now, compare your list with the
     author's words and discuss why you
     think the author has chosen the words
     that he has.
3 'The sunny slow lulling afternoon yawns
   and moons through the dozy town.'
   'Clouds sag and pillow on Llaregyb Hill.'
   Try and describe what the author wants
   us to imagine as we read these lines.

Your own writing

Use the first sentence of the extract from
Under Milk Wood to begin a paragraph in
which you describe a sleepy, deserted town
centre on a hot day, with the shops shut.
Imagine what it would be like, then try to
continue this sleepy trance-like atmosphere.

Taking it further

Choose one of the following settings:
- a place of imprisonment
- a place of security
- a place of magic and power
- a place of desolation and decay
- a place of loneliness
- a place of secrecy

Visualize a specific place and list the details
you want to include. As you write, try and
evoke a particular mood, including the effect
this setting has on your character.

A Room of Your Own

A room can tell you a lot about a person. Consider your own room. What would a stranger deduce about you from a five minute study?

Revealing character

On your own, read the piece below and then listen to it read aloud. As you are listening to the second reading, jot down what kind of person you can see living here. What is their age and background? How do they feel about their surroundings?

Try and find particular words and phrases to support your ideas.

Goggle Eyes

Kitty's mum's new boyfriend has been making himself very much at home in their house. Her mother and sister welcome this, but Kitty despises him. He has offered to find an airlock in the pipes and has ventured into Kitty's room.

He flung the curtains open. Light flooded the room.

There was stunned silence, then:

'Dear gods!' he whispered softly in some awe. 'Designer compost!'

He gazed about him in amazement. And it did look a bit slummy, I admit. Blackened banana skins don't look too nasty dropped in a waste paper basket, but when you see them spread on your crumpled bedclothes, coated with cat hairs, they can be a bit off-putting. And the tops were off most of the make-up and hair stuff. And the playing cards would have looked neater in a pile. And if my dresser drawers had been pushed in, none of my underwear would have been spilling on the floor.

He stopped to pick up a mug with two inches of stone cold coffee inside it, and a layer of thick green scum over the top.

'Interesting,' he said. 'Bit of a rarity, this particular mould.'

'I think you mentioned an airlock in our pipes,' I said coldly.

Notice that? Not *the* pipes. *Our* pipes. I always hoped that if I managed to make him sound enough like a trespasser in our house, he might go away. It never worked.

'Oh, yes.'

He made a space for the coffee cup on my desk, between my furry slippers and a large tin of cat food I must have brought up from downstairs one night when Floss seemed hungry. Brushing aside a tell-tale nest of crinkly wrappers from the last box of chocolates he'd brought to the house, he knelt down on the floor.

'Do you mind if I prise a few of these odd socks out from behind your radiator?' he asked politely. 'Principles of convection, you understand.'

'*I'll* get them out.'

I wouldn't have seemed so keen to cooperate, but you know how it is when someone starts rooting around the more impenetrable areas of your bedroom. You never know if they're going to turn up something so embarrassing you'll *die* of shame.

As I reached in the top of the radiator, he tapped the bottom sharply. Two shrivelled apple cores shot out.

He frowned.

He tapped the radiator again, a little harder. Another apple core shot out, stuck to a chocolate that I didn't like much, and there was a rich-sounding gurgle as water welled freely along the pipes for the first time in days.

'There.' He sat back on his heels. 'I think that might well be the problem solved.'

Brushing green eye-glitter from the knees of his trousers, he stood and took one more slow, marvelling look around my room. His eyes, I noticed, came to rest on my pot plant.

'Fascinating,' he said. 'Look at it. No water. No fresh air. No sunlight. And still it lives.'

'Is that it?' I asked coldly. 'Are you finished?'

He turned and pulled the door back as far as it would go against my heap of English books.

'Miss Kitty Killin,' he said admiringly, edging as best he could through the narrow gap. 'The only girl in the whole world who can make litter out of literature!'

Before I could stick out my tongue at him, he had gone.

Anne Fine

Your own writing

1 Describe your own room so a reader can see the kind of person you are by what surrounds you. Then share your work with a partner: what does the description reveal about you?

2 Choose a particular occupation or lifestyle, and without revealing the identity of your person, describe their surroundings using the following format:

■ you are standing at a window: what do you see outside?
■ you turn back into the room: what surrounds you?
■ someone enters the room: who are they and how do you react to them?

Get your partner to read what you have written. Who do they think your person is? What details were most effective? Use their ideas to improve your piece.

Horror!
What Makes a Good Horror Story?

Just what are the essential ingredients of a good horror story?
What kind of scenery or setting might it have?
What kind of characters would appear in the story?
What kind of events might happen?

Talking it through

Below are a number of personal opinions from both authors
and students about what makes a good ghost or horror story.
In groups of four, read them through.

1 Are there any other points that you would add? Make a
  note of them. Be prepared to justify your own personal
  ideas in discussion and use examples from books you
  have read and films you have seen.

2 See if you can agree on a rank order for these points,
  running from most important to least important.

Adele Geras

'There should still be some kind of mystery at the end so you think the story is not quite over.'

'The writer should build up suspense bit by bit so you're hanging on the edge of your seat.'

'To have the evil come from an unexpected place.'

'Things should happen in places you could see or visit so you believe it could happen to you.'

'You should begin to care about one of the characters so you're bothered about what happens to them.'

'I try and release ghosts from their gothic sets and relocate them in the modern world.'

'...To create a sense of uncertainty, foreboding and a threat of perpetual attack...'

John Christopher

'I try to describe and evoke the setting and the details as well as I can... they are what makes the difference between the merely routine and the really memorable.'

Adele Geras

A typical horror story

Read the three extracts below from horror writing.

1 Working in pairs, use the ideas you have just discussed, and the table below, to try and decide:

- what kind of places horror stories usually occur in
- what kind of people are usually involved
- what kind of key incidents are likely

Enter your findings in a table similar to the one below. It has been started for you, using part of the Adele Geras extract.

INGREDIENTS IN A TYPICAL GHOST/HORROR STORY	
SETTING	A forbidden room that is usually out of bounds
CHARACTER	Someone disturbed by what they see, in danger of being caught but fascinated and needing to explore
EVENTS	Building/creating of character from other people's bodies – here it is dolls
POSSIBLE TITLES TO READ	'Point Horror' books

2 As a class, share your findings from the table.
3 With the comments by writers and students in mind, discuss which of the extracts you found the least chilling and why you think this is.

The Dollmaker

Ruth opened the door. It was a very small room, only a boxroom, really. There was a table pushed up against the window. On the walls there were hooks: hundreds of them, and hanging from the hooks were arms and legs and even bald dolls' heads with empty eye sockets, dangling in such a way as to make them seem alive, like bits of very small children. There was a shelf stacked with limbless bodies, plastic torsos waiting. Waiting to be made whole. Another shelf had small wigs balanced on rows and rows of little sticks. A large biscuit tin lay open on the table, and Ruth went to look into it and drew back quickly. That's horrible, she thought, and then: how silly I am. It's only eyes… bits of plastic and glass, that's all. But the way they stared up at her, hard and unblinking and the way they just seemed about to roll around, or move, and all their different colours… She left the room and closed the door behind her.

Adele Geras

25

Frankenstein

It was on a dreary night of November that I beheld the accomplishment of my toils. With an anxiety that almost amounted to agony, I collected the instruments of life around me, that I might infuse a spark of being into the lifeless thing that lay at my feet. It was already one in the morning; the rain pattered dismally against the panes, and my candle was nearly burnt out, when, by the glimmer of the half-extinguished light, I saw the dull yellow eye of the creature open; it breathed hard, and a convulsive motion agitated its limbs.

How can I describe my emotions at this catastrophe, or how delineate the wretch whom with such infinite pains and care I had endeavoured to form? His limbs were in proportion, and I had selected his features as beautiful. Beautiful! Great God! His yellow skin scarcely covered the work of muscles and arteries beneath; his hair was of a lustrous black, and flowing; his teeth of a pearly whiteness; but these luxuriances only formed a more horrid contrast with his watery eyes, that seemed almost of the same colour as the dun-white sockets in which they were set, his shrivelled complexion and straight black lips.

The different accidents of life are not so changeable as the feelings of human nature. I had worked hard for nearly two years, for the sole purpose of infusing life into an inanimate body. For this I had deprived myself of rest and health. I had desired it with an ardour that far exceeded moderation; but now that I had finished, the beauty of the dream vanished, and breathless horror and disgust filled my heart.

Mary Shelley

A Light in the Black

The lights were on the train.

They were moving along the cars towards them. That's why they were growing, coming nearer. He'd thought the wagons were hurtling towards the light, but the train was hardly moving at all now. How many lights? How many Cyclops-eyed creatures? He tried to count. Twelve, thirteen, fourteen. Fourteen blinding, staring eyes; fourteen hunched and moving figures.

No, he thought, no, this was insane, impossible. He was trying to shut out his thoughts, but all he could hear now was Dave Brookman's voice closing slowly over his mind:

He could raise the dead if he needed to…

And, Jesus, he could too. He could and he *had*. And he'd always said he was capable of anything. So now he knew what Stands could do; he knew it, and didn't want to know it. But, with the gloating lights almost upon them, it was Steve who asked the question he hadn't wanted to ask himself.

'How many? How many miners in that flooded-out shaft?'

Steve was holding a five-pound hammer aloft, but he didn't seem sure what to do with it. It wavered in his hand like rubber. 'But why? Why'd he have to go so far?'

'Because it's what you all wanted,' said a voice, behind them.

They wheeled around to look, hearts in mouths.

'You and the others in town,' said the voice, invisible, from the darkest part of the Dark Place. 'The wives who wished them alive again. The dabbling old fools like Ruth who wanted to see life after life. That's what you all wanted, isn't it?' The dimmest, grimmest chuckle and then, 'You wanted your mine to be rich again, so look! I made it rich! You wanted your dead to walk again, and look! I got them walking!'

The shadow-man's high whooping laugh filled the tunnel.

The lights of the walking miners drew nearer, huddling around.

Then, without speaking, they were stumbling free of the paddy-car and down to the rasp and squelch of the roadway floor, Jules with his hand growing numb in Rachel's, Steve with his clanking rucksack, the hammer at his side. They stood there with nowhere to turn, walled in by laughter, walled in by dead, breathing miners.

Chris Westwood

Taking it further

1 Look at one or more ghost/horror stories. How many of the 'typical ingredients' you have listed appear? What are the untypical elements? Do these untypical elements make the story more gripping, or less successful?

2 Write a brief for a would-be horror story writer, giving advice on the elements to include in a horror story.

What Happened Next?

Using all the knowledge you have built up so far about how horror stories work, in pairs see if you can predict what is going to happen in the following story.

(As you read, you will notice that four different artists have illustrated this story. This relates to an activity at the end of the unit.)

Predicting from the title

The title is *The Call*. What do you think is going to happen?

Now together, listen to extract 1 as it is read to you.

The Call

1 I'm rota-secretary of our local Samaritans. My job's to see our office is staffed twenty-four hours a day, 365 days a year. It's a load of headaches, I can tell you. And the worst headache for any branch is overnight on Christmas Eve.

Eighteen fruitless phone-calls later, I got somebody. Meg and Geoff Charlesworth. Just married; no kids.

When they came in at ten to relieve me, they were happy. Maybe they'd had a couple of drinks in the course of the evening. They were laughing; but they were certainly fit to drive. It is wrong to accuse them, as some did, later, of having had too many. Meg gave me a Christmas kiss. She'd wound a bit of silver tinsel through her hair, as some girls do at Christmas. They'd brought long red candles to light, and mince-pies to heat up in our kitchen and eat at midnight. It was just happiness; and it *was* Christmas Eve.

Then my wife tooted our car-horn outside, and I passed out of the story. The rest is hearsay; from the log they kept, and the reports they wrote, that were still lying in the in-tray the following morning.

The time

In your pair, suggest why the author decided to set his story on Christmas Eve.

2 They heard the distant bells of the parish church, filtering through the falling snow, announcing midnight. Meg got the mince-pies out of the oven, and Geoff was just kissing her, mouth full of flaky pastry, when the emergency phone went.

Being young and keen, they both grabbed for it. Meg won. Geoff shook his fist at her silently, and dutifully logged the call. Midnight exactly, according to his new watch.

He heard Meg say what she'd been carefully coached to say, like Samaritans the world over.

'Samaritans – can I help you?'

She said it just right. Warm, but not gushing. Interested, but not *too* interested. That first phrase is all-important. Say it wrong, the client rings off without speaking.

Meg frowned. She said the phrase again. Geoff crouched close in support, trying to catch what he could from Meg's ear-piece. He said afterwards the line was very bad. Crackly, very crackly. Nothing but crackles, coming and going.

Meg said her phrase the third time. She gestured to Geoff that she wanted a chair. He silently got one, pushed it in behind her knees. She began to wind her fingers into the coiled telephone-cord, like all Samaritans do when they're anxious.

Meg said into the phone, 'I'd like to help if I can.' It was good to vary the phrase, otherwise clients began to think you were a tape-recording. She added, 'My name's Meg. What can I call *you*?' You never ask for their real name, at that stage; always what you can call them. Often they start off by giving a false name…

A voice spoke through the crackle. A female voice.

'He's going to kill me. I know he's going to kill me. When he comes back.' Geoff, who caught it from a distance, said it wasn't the phrases that were so awful. It was the way they were said.

Cold; so cold. And certain. It left no doubt in your mind he *would* come back and kill her. It wasn't a wild voice you could hope to calm down. It wasn't a cunning hysterical voice, trying to upset you. It wasn't the voice of a hoaxer, that to the trained Samaritan ear always has that little wobble in it, that might break down into a giggle at any minute and yet, till it does, must be taken absolutely seriously. Geoff said it was a voice as cold, as real, as hopeless as a tombstone.

'Why do you think he's going to kill you?' Geoff said Meg's voice was shaking, but only a little. Still warm, still interested.

Silence. Crackle.

'Has he *threatened* you?'

When the voice came again, it wasn't an answer to her question. It was another chunk of lonely hell, being spat out automatically; as if the woman at the other end was really only talking to herself.

'He's gone to let a boat through the lock. When he comes back, he's going to kill me.'

Meg's voice tried to go up an octave; she caught it just in time.

'Has he *threatened* you? What is he going to do?'

'He's goin' to push me in the river, so it looks like an accident.'

'Can't you swim?'

'There's half an inch of ice on the water. Nobody could live a minute.'

'Can't you get away… before he comes back?'

'Nobody lives within miles. And I'm lame.'

'Can't I… you… ring the police?'

Geoff heard a click, as the line went dead. The dialling tone resumed. Meg put the phone down wearily, and suddenly shivered, though the office was over-warm, from the roaring gas-fire.

'Christ, I'm so *cold*!'

Geoff brought her cardigan, and put it round her. 'Shall I ring the duty-director, or will you?'

'You. If you heard it all.'

Tom Brett came down the line, brisk and cheerful. 'I've not gone to bed yet. Been filling the little blighter's Christmas stocking…'

Geoff gave him the details. Tom Brett was everything a good duty-director should be. Listened without interrupting; came back solid and reassuring as a house.

'Boats don't go through the locks this time of night. Haven't done for twenty years. The old alkali steamers used to, when the alkali-trade was

30

still going strong. The locks are only manned nine till five nowadays. Pleasure-boats can wait till morning. As if anyone would be moving a pleasure-boat this weather…'

'Are you *sure*?' asked Geoff doubtfully.

'Quite sure. Tell you something else – the river's nowhere near freezing over. Runs past my back-fence. Been watching it all day, 'cos I bought the lad a fishing-rod for Christmas, and it's not much fun if he can't try it out. You've been *had*, old son. Some Christmas joker having you on. Goodnight!'

'Hoax call,' said Geoff heavily, putting the phone down. 'No boats going through locks. No ice on the river. Look!' He pulled back the curtain from the office window. 'It's still quite warm out – the snow's melting, not even lying.'

Meg looked at the black wet road, and shivered again. 'That was no hoax. Did you think that voice was a hoax?'

'We'll do what the boss-man says. Ours not to reason why…'

He was still waiting for the kettle to boil, when the emergency phone went again.

The first phone call

1 What effect does the caller have on Meg?
2 Why does the call appear to be a hoax?
3 Why are Meg and Geoff unsure about what to do next?
4 Who will be on the phone this time and what do you think will happen?

 The same voice.

'But he *can't* just push you in the river and get away with it!' said Meg desperately.

'He can. I always take the dog for a walk last thing. And there's places where the bank is crumbling and the fence's rotting. And the fog's coming down. He'll break a bit of fence, then put the leash on the dog, and throw it in after me. Doesn't matter whether the dog drowns or is found wanderin'.

Either'll suit *him.* Then he'll ring the police an' say I'm missin'…

'But why should he *want* to? What've you *done*? To deserve it?'

'I'm gettin' old. I've got a bad leg. I'm not much use to him. He's got a new bit o' skirt down the village…'

'But can't we…'

'All you can do for me, love, is to keep me company till he comes. It's lonely… That's not much to ask, is it?'

'Where *are* you?'

Geoff heard the line go dead again. He thought Meg looked like a corpse herself. White as a sheet. Dull dead eyes, full of pain. Ugly, almost. How she would look as an old woman, if life was rough on her.

'I want to know where she *is*. I want to know where she's ringing from…'

To placate her, Geoff got out the large-scale Ordnance-Survey maps that some offices carry. It wasn't a great problem. The Ousam was a rarity; the only canalized river with locks for fifty miles around. And there were only eight sets of locks on it.

'These four,' said Geoff, 'are right in the middle of towns and villages. So it can't be *them*. And there's a whole row of Navigation cottages at Sutton's Lock, and I know they're occupied, so it can't be *there*. And this last one – Ousby Point – is right on the sea and it's all docks and stone quays – there's no river-bank to crumble. So it's either Yaxton Bridge, or Moresby Abbey locks…'

The emergency phone rang again. There is a myth among old Samaritans that you can tell the quality of the incoming call by the sound of the phone-bell. Sometimes it's lonely, sometimes cheerful, sometimes downright frantic. Nonsense, of course. A bell is a bell is a bell…

But this ringing sounded so cold, so dreary, so dead, that for a second they both hesitated and looked at each other with dread. Then Meg slowly picked the phone up; like a bather hesitating on the bank of a cold grey river.

It was the voice again.

'The boat's gone through. He's just closing the lock gates. He'll be here in a minute…'

'What kind of boat is it?' asked Meg, with a desperate attempt at self-defence.

Geoff took one look at his wife's grey, frozen, horrified face, and snatched the phone from her hand. He might be a Samaritan; but he was a husband, too. He wasn't sitting and watching his wife being screwed by some vicious hoaxer.

'Now *look*!' he said. 'Whoever you are! –'

The line went dead.

'Oh, *Geoff!*' said Meg.

'Sorry. But the moment I called her bluff, she rang off.'

Meg's reaction

What effect is the caller beginning to have on Meg now?

Between extracts 3 and 4 Geoff drives out to check Ousby Locks, where everything is fine. Terrified for his wife's safety he dashes back to base to find her, cold with terror, clutching the telephone. He grabs the phone, which immediately goes dead. His wife turns to him and says:

4 'Her husband was in the house. He was just about to open the door where she was…'

'Did you find out where she was?'

'Moresby Abbey lock. She told me in the end. I got her confidence. Then *you* came and ruined it…'

She said it as if he was suddenly her enemy. An enemy, a fool, a bully, a murderer. Like all men. Then she said, 'I must go to her…'

'And leave the office unattended? That's *mad.*' He took off his coat with the car-keys, and hung it on the office door. He came back and looked at her again. She still seemed a bit odd, trance-like. But she smiled at him and said, 'Make me a quick cup of tea. I must go to the loo, before she rings again.'

Glad they were friends again, he went and put the kettle on. Stood impatiently waiting for it to boil, tapping his fingers on the sink-unit, trying to work out what they should do. He heard Meg's step in the hallway. Heard the toilet flush.

Then he heard a car start up outside.

His car.

He rushed out into the hall. The front door was swinging, letting in the snow. Where his car had been, there were only tyre-marks.

He was terrified now. Not for the woman. For Meg.

He rang Tom Brett, more frightened than any client Tom Brett had ever heard.

He told Tom what he knew.

'Moresby Locks,' said Tom. 'A lame woman. A murdering husband. Oh, my God. I'll be with you in five.'

The caller's identity

1 Who do you think is calling?
2 What is she trying to do?
3 Why is Tom so terrified?

5 'The exchange are putting emergency calls through to Jimmy Henry,' said Tom, peering through the whirling wet flakes that were clogging his windscreen-wipers. 'Do you know what way Meg was getting to Moresby Locks?'

'The only way,' said Geoff. 'Park at Wylop Bridge and walk a mile up the towpath.'

'There's a short cut. Down through the woods by the Abbey, and over the lock-gates. Not a lot of people know about it. I think we'll take that one. I want to get there before she does…'

'What the hell do you think is going on?'

'I've got an *idea*. But if I told you, you'd think I was out of my tiny shiny. So I won't. All I want is your Meg safe and dry, back in the Sam. office. And nothing in the log that headquarters might see…'

He turned off the by-pass, into the narrow track where hawthorn bushes reached out thorny arms and scraped at the paintwork of the car. After a long while, he grunted with satisfaction, clapped on the brakes and said, 'Come on.'

They ran across the narrow wooden walkway that sat precariously on top of the lock-gates. The flakes of snow whirled at them, in the light of Tom's torch. Behind the gates, the water stacked up, black, smooth, slightly steaming because it was warmer than the air. In an evil way, it called to Geoff. So easy to slip in, let the icy arms embrace you, slip away…

Then they were over, on the towpath. They looked left, right, listened.

Footsteps, woman's footsteps, to the right. They ran that way. Geoff saw Meg's walking back, in its white raincoat…

And beyond Meg, leading Meg, another back, another woman's back. The back of a woman who limped.

A woman with a dog. A little white dog…

For some reason, neither of them called out to Meg. Fear of disturbing a Samaritan relationship, perhaps. Fear of breaking up something that neither of them understood. After all, they could afford to be patient now. They had found Meg safe. They were closing up quietly on her, only ten yards away. No danger…

The conclusion

What do you think will happen next?

6 Then, in the light of Tom's torch, a break in the white-painted fence on the river side.

And the figure of the limping woman turned through the gap in the fence, and walked out over the still black waters of the river.

And like a sleepwalker, Meg turned to follow…

They caught her on the very brink. Each of them caught her violently by one arm, like policemen arresting a criminal. Tom cursed, as one of his feet slipped down the bank and into the water. But he held on to them, as they all swayed on the brink, and he only got one very wet foot.

'What the hell am I doing here?' asked Meg, as if waking from a dream. 'She was talking to me. I'd got her confidence…'

'Did she tell you her name?'

'Agnes Todd.'

'Well,' said Tom, 'here's where Agnes Todd used to live.'

There were only low walls of stone, in the shape of a house. With stretches of concrete and old broken tile in between. There had been a phone, because there was still a telegraph pole, with a broken junction-box from which two black wires flapped like flags in the wind.

'Twenty-one years ago, Reg Todd kept this lock. His lame wife Agnes lived with him. They didn't get on well – people passing the cottage heard them quarrelling. Christmas Eve, 1964, he reported her missing to the police. She'd gone out for a walk with the dog, and not come back. The police searched. There was a bad fog down that night. They found a hole in the railing, just about where we saw one; and a hole in the ice, just glazing over. They found the dog's body next day; but they didn't find her for a month, till the ice on the River Ousam finally broke up.

'The police tried to make a case of it. Reg Todd *had* been carrying on with a girl in the village. But there were no marks of violence. In the end, she could have fallen, she could've been pushed, or she could've jumped. So they let Reg Todd go; and he left the district.'

There was a long silence. Then Geoff said, 'So you think…?'

'I think nowt,' said Tom Brett, suddenly very stubborn and solid and Fenman. 'I think nowt, and that's all I *know*. Now let's get your missus home.'

Robert Westall

Clues to the end

1 If you guessed right, what clues did the author give that helped you?

2 How do you see the ending? Discuss with a partner which of the following possible interpretations seems most likely.

■ The ghost is simply repeating past events
■ The ghost is a victim appealing for help
■ The ghost is evil and is trying to kill Meg
(At the end, Meg comes to 'as if waking from a dream.' What does this suggest?)

The Publishing Business

For the following game you will need to work in groups of five. Your group will become the editorial team in a publishing house, deciding whether to publish Robert Westall's story, *The Call*, as the title story in a collection of horror stories for eleven- to thirteen-year-olds. Each person will take on one of the following roles:

1 Publisher – also chairperson
2 Editor
3 Designer
4 Sales Manager
5 Publicity Manager

You will each be issued with a card which explains your responsibilities. However, all decisions taken have to be discussed with the group first.

How to play

1 The game begins with the publisher reading the publishing proposal printed below.

2 Everyone then rereads *The Call* and their ideas on what makes a good horror story.

3 Each person is then issued with their role cards. In turn, beginning with the publisher, each person reads out their card and the group discuss the problems they have to solve.

4 After everyone has had a chance to put their side of the argument, the players can vote on whether or not they want to publish the story. The publisher listens to all views and makes the final decision if the other votes 'for' and 'against' are equal.

There is not necessarily a right or wrong answer – publishing houses would make different decisions.

PUBLISHING PROPOSAL FOR *THE CALL*

(To be read aloud by the publisher)

We want to expand our Teenage Horror books so that we compete with other publishing houses and attract teenage readers. Our aim in this discussion is to decide if this story is strong enough to be the first story in a collection of ghost stories. The collection will be sold first as a hardback at £12.99 each, and then as a paperback at £5.99. The author, Robert Westall, has written a number of successful books.

36

Publishing 'The Call'

The clip you are about to see shows interviews with the publishing team which produced and marketed *The Young Oxford Book of Ghost Stories* – a collection which features Robert Westall's story *The Call.*

Listen carefully to all the comments they make, but particularly to those that relate to your specific role. (If you are the designer, the illustrator's comments may suggest things to bear in mind when choosing an artist.)

Make a note of any additional ideas, hints, or guidelines that these experts give about the areas you will want to consider.

Try to refer to these comments as you discuss your own ideas in your group.

Publicity: Vanessa Doughty

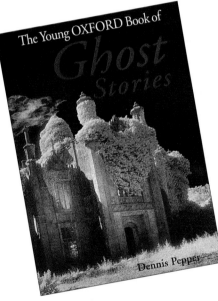

The book

Sales: Phil Garratt

Editor: Ron Heapy

Illustrator: Ian Miller

Publisher

I am responsible for running this meeting and ensuring that, as a group, we come up with a final decision that everyone has played their part in. I will be listening to everyone's views, encouraging everyone to have their say and stopping any one person from taking over the debate. If there is a split decision at the end, I will have the casting vote. I will also be responsible for reporting our findings back to my superiors [the rest of the class].

Editor

I am responsible for deciding what kind of book this will be, and what stories should go into it to ensure it will sell well.

Discussion questions

1 Is this type of story popular?
2 Is it well-written? Are the characters believable? Does it contain the ingredients of a good horror story?
3 Would teenagers enjoy reading it?
4 Is the author well-known? (See Sheet A.)
5 What other similar books are available?

Designer

I am responsible for the look of the book, including the illustrations and the page design. For instance, very different designs would be needed for a reference book and a picture book.

Discussion questions

1 Which artist will you choose to illustrate this particular story? (See the different styles of artwork on pages 28–35.)
2 Should the illustrations be in colour or black and white?

Sales Manager

I visit schools, libraries and bookshops to get orders for the book. I have to work out if the price is right and how many copies can be sold.

Discussion questions

1 Who will buy this book? Children or their parents, teachers or librarians?
2 Is the price correct?
3 Which of the above groups are more likely to buy the paperback and which the hardback?

Publicity Manager

I have to make sure that possible buyers are aware of the book. I have to produce an Advance Information Sheet telling buyers what is special about this title. I organize special publicity material, place advertisements and run special events like competitions, bookshop displays, or a party to celebrate the launch of the book.

Discussion questions

1 What is the best way to attract the attention of the people you think will buy this book?
2 Would you produce any special publicity material to promote the book?
3 What information would you put on an Advance Information Sheet?

Taking it further

In your group, you have used your knowledge of horror stories to decide whether or not to publish the Robert Westall story in your anthology. However, you still need between ten and fifteen other short horror stories to complete the collection. Dividing the class into two groups of readers and writers, individually you should complete one of the following tasks:

1 Readers

In your group, each pick out one or two stories from the following collections or from your own reading. You will be responsible for reading these. Then, using your knowledge of what makes a good horror story, prepare a short report on your stories stating whether or not you would use them in an anthology, and why. As a whole group you can then recommend ten good horror short stories to the rest of the class.

Robert Westall
The Call and Other Stories
(Penguin Plus)

Adele Geras
The Lane to the Land of the Dead
(Hamish Hamilton)

Jean Russell (ed.)
The Dollmaker and Other Stories
(Mammoth Books)

Chris Westwood
Any title
(Penguin Plus)

Dennis Pepper (ed.)
The Young Oxford Book of Ghost Stories
(Oxford University Press)

Edgar Allan Poe
Tales of Mystery and Imagination
(Pan Books)

2 Writers

Write a short horror story of between 500 and 1000 words that could be considered for your class anthology. To help you, aim to include some of the key ingredients below:

- an opening paragraph that sets the scene, e.g. a lonely house or a lonely evening when few people will be out
- some sort of omen or prediction of what will happen, e.g. an old painting, a face at a window, a strange message or a well-known local tale about a strange happening
- some sort of reaction from your character, e.g. anger, alarm, or terror
- a series of connected events that offer small clues to the reader, e.g. the telephone call with a little more detail in each call
- a building of suspense through setting, events, and your characters' reactions. Try using senses like smell, hearing, and sight to make your character frightened – e.g. the sound of the telephone or the apparition by the river
- a final climax followed by the tale of some event in the past that explains what has happened

When you have finished, you could ask the other group of readers to decide which stories should be used in your class anthology.

Language Study

Writing in Non-Standard English

Gary Paulsen's novel *Nightjohn* is based on his research into the lives of American slaves in the eighteenth and nineteenth centuries. Because he is telling the story through the eyes of a slave girl called Sarny, he uses her dialect which is based upon the 'creole' language spoken in the British slave colonies.

Here is a continuation of the extract on pages 9–10.

He come in bad and it wasn't until late that night, after
60 dark in the quarters, that I learned his name.

Mammy she made canvas pants for the new men when they came. Sewed them from the roll of tarp-cloth we used for all our clothes. She gave a pair to Nightjohn when they came in from the field but he didn't have time to say nothing because it was time for the evening food…

The slaves sleep as soon as they have eaten. But the new man is different:

He didn't even get on the floor but went right over to the corner where mammy put the pot to pray sometimes and sat there. The new canvas pants were so stiff I could hear them crackle and bend when he sat back against the wall.
70 I was on the side of mammy's shuck mattress along with about half a dozen young ones who were all kicking and scratching so sleep wasn't coming and I hear:

'Who's got tobacco? I need some tobacco.'

It was a whisper, but loud, cutting from the corner where the new man sat. I had me some tobacco. It was just shredded bottom leaf that I'd been chewing to spit on the roses but I'd kept some back in a wrapped piece of sacking inside my shirtdress, tied round my waist on a piece of string. I didn't say a word. You come on things,
80 things to keep, and you keep them to trade for other things. Things you need. Like pork fat. Or pennies.

He chuckled, low and rippling. Sounded like a low wind through willows, that small laugh, or maybe water moving over round rocks. Deep and soft.

'I'll trade,' he whispered. 'I'll trade something for a lip of tobacco.'

I thought, What you got to trade? You come in naked as the day you was born, come in bad with whip marks up

40

90 and down your back, not even a set of clothes or canvas pants and you're ready to go to trading? I didn't say it, but I thought it. And he like to read my thoughts.

'What I got to trade, what I got to trade for a lip of tobacco is letters. I knows letters. I'll trade *A*, *B*, and *C* for a lip of chew.' He laughed again.

And there I was, with the tobacco in my dress and he said that and I didn't know what letters was, nor what they meant, but I thought it might be something I wanted to know. To learn.

Gary Paulsen

To help you to pick out some of the features of Sarny's dialect and learn how it differs from standard English, complete the following table, filling in whichever of the two dialect forms is missing. You will need to refer to the beginning of the extract (on pages 9–10) and the continuation on these pages.

Standard English dialect	Sarny's non-standard dialect
1 Verbs	
	like he *be* a big man (l. 19)
	they*'s* two men he calls drivers (l. 41)
	they *be* hungry (l. 56)
the day you *were* born (l. 88)	
	I *knows* letters (l. 93)
I didn't know what letters *were* (l. 96)	
2 Grammar	
	Mammy she made canvas pants (l. 61)
didn't have time to say *anything* (l.64)	
if they don't do it all (l. 40)	
	there *ain't never* enough (l. 56)
What have you got to trade? (l. 87)	
I had some tobacco (l. 75)	
3 Vocabulary	
corn-husk (l. 58)	
trousers (l. 61)	
	shirtdress (l. 78)

Direct and Reported Speech

Writers such as Robert Westall, the author of *The Call*, usually find it more effective to give the reader the exact words that the characters speak. For example, the character Tom Brett says:

'Boats don't go through the locks this time of night.'

When we write down the speaker's actual words, we are using **direct speech**.

Sometimes, though, a writer will decide to report what the character said, rather than give the actual words. Robert Westall might have written:

Tom Brett said that boats *didn't* go through the locks *that* time of night.

Notice the two differences:

■ *don't* (in the present tense) becomes *didn't* (in the past tense)

■ *this time* becomes *that time*

How would the following pieces of direct speech look if they were in **reported speech**?

1 'I'll trade,' he whispered. (from *Nightjohn*, page 40)
   Begin: He whispered that...

2 'You've grown,' he said... (from *Dear Mr Henshaw*, page 14)
   (Begin: He said that I...)

3 'Is that it?' I asked coldly. (from *Goggle Eyes*, page 23)
   (Begin: I asked coldly whether...)

Which particular changes did you make in each case? Can you begin to make up some 'rules' about changing from direct speech into reported speech?

Direct speech in narrative

Why do you think writers of stories nearly always use direct speech rather than reported speech? Look at the following extracts and, in pairs, decide what advantages there are in having the characters' exact words, rather than a report of what they said.

■ *Dear Mr Henshaw*, page 12, from 'Did you leave the door open for him?' to How could he?

■ *Treasure Island*, page 19, from 'I've taken a notion...' to '...Tom Morgan?'

■ *Goggle Eyes*, page 22, from 'Interesting,' he said... to 'Oh, yes.'

■ *A Light in the Black*, page 27, from 'How many?...', to 'I got them walking!'

■ *The Call*, page 30, from When the voice came again... to ...as the line went dead.

There is more on direct and reported speech on pages 154–155.

Nouns

As you learned in Book 1, nouns are a class of words which label people, places, things, or ideas. If a noun labels a *particular* person, place or thing, it is called a **proper noun** and will begin with a capital letter. Most other nouns are **common nouns**.

The extract from *Dear Mr Henshaw* on page 14 contains examples of common nouns and proper nouns:

Proper nouns labelling a particular place or person

'Since it wasn't far, I thought I'd take a run over here before I take off for Ohio.'

So Dad had come to see me just because of broccoli. After all these months when I had longed to see him, it took a load of broccoli to get him here. I felt let down and my feelings hurt.

Common noun labelling a thing

There are two other types of noun in this short extract.

Abstract nouns

Look first at the words 'months' and 'feelings'. This kind of noun is called an **abstract noun**, and is the label we give to things we cannot see or touch, such as emotions, thoughts or ideas. (*Abstract* means to do with ideas, rather than objects.)

1 Which abstract nouns label the following *times*:
   - a period of ten years
   - a period of a thousand years
   - a hundredth anniversary?

2 Which abstract nouns label the *feeling* you have when:
   - you need something to eat
   - you are doing something that doesn't interest you
   - you are opening a present?

3 Which abstract nouns might label the *qualities* you need to be a successful
   - player of computer games
   - dancer
   - writer?

Forming abstract nouns from adjectives

Many abstract nouns are formed very simply by adding *-ness* to an adjective:
   e.g. *bright*ness, *open*ness, *sad*ness.
If the adjective ends in a *-y*, it changes to an *i* when *-ness* is added:
   e.g. *happy* + ness becomes *happi*ness.
In pairs, brainstorm as many abstract nouns as you can which are made up of an adjective ending in *-y*, plus *-ness*. Put them in brief sentences, or try to use them all in a short paragraph.

Forming abstract nouns from verbs

Abstract nouns are often formed from verbs by changing the ending of the verb or adding a suffix:
   e.g. the verb deci*de* gives the abstract noun deci*sion*.

Which abstract nouns are formed from *complain, state, compete, solve, relate*?

Collective nouns

The fourth kind of noun is called a **collective noun**.

An example of this from the extract is 'load'. Collective nouns are the labels we give to *groups* or *collections* of people, animals or things. A lorry's load is its cargo (another collective noun). Other common examples include words such as 'herd', 'team', and 'set'.

1 What are the collective nouns normally used to label the following animals when they are in groups?
   - fish
   - sheep
   - geese

2 What do you have a *sheaf* of?

3 What would grow in a *tuft*, and what in a *clump*?

4 What can you have a *fleet* of, apart from boats?

5 How many different things can you have a *flight* of?

6 What do you find in an *anthology*?

Poem as Story

Limericks

There was a young farmer from Leeds
Who swallowed a packet of seeds
In a month, silly ass,
He was covered in grass,
And he couldn't sit down for the weeds.

Maybe the search for food
Maybe a quest for glory,
But write a poem
With a story.

Adrian Mitchell

There was a young lady from Ickenham
Who went on a bus trip to Twickenham
She drank too much beer
Which made her feel queer
So she took off her boots and was sick in 'em.

Recipe for a limerick

A limerick poem tells a short story that is funny and rhymes.

1 In pairs take a look at the two limericks above and see if you can
   explain more clearly just how a limerick works. Try and write a recipe
   for a limerick that might include:
   - the number of lines
   - what a limerick is usually about
   - which lines rhyme
   - how many beats you get in a line
   - how many syllables you get in a line

2 When you have decided on your recipe, share it as a class. Note down
   the main points, then see if you can use your recipe to untangle the
   four limericks on the next page. Try working by yourself and then
   sharing your results with a partner.

Said a boastful young student from Hays

'My tunnel's superb it can't fail.'

Through April and May

There was a young man from Bengal

Dressed up as a bun

He's been missing for forty-three days.

He went just for fun

Dad waited while Mum bought the ham

'There's nothing in it,

But when she came out she said, 'Sam!

But look it's a much better pram.'

Who went to a fancy dress ball

Said a convict in prison in Sale

That one's not our baby!'

As he entered the Hampton Court Maze

And a dog ate him up in the hall.

I'll be back in a minute.'

Then came up inside Brixton Jail.

He dug night and day

He answered, 'Well maybe,

Writing your own

Once you have discovered how a limerick works, try experimenting with your own.

1 In a group of five, find as many rhymes as you can for the following places: Deal, Crewe, Spain, Ryde, Slough, York, Leeds, Poole, Wales, Crawley, Brighton and Bristol.

2 Using your chosen rhymes, take one town or country each and try composing Consequence Limericks.

■ Each person writes the opening line to a limerick.

■ Without folding the piece of paper down, he or she then passes it on to the next person.

■ The next person adds the next line, and passes it on again. The limerick will come back completed to the person who started it and they should then read it out. The most successful limerick in the group can be shared with the class.

3 Finally, in a pair you can devise your own limericks. You can either write new opening lines or use the rhymes explored in your group. Completed limericks could be entered in a class anthology entitled, 'There was a young person from …'

Opening Up

The next poem tells the story of a present and what the present means to the writer. As you read it, it is easy to picture the objects and events being described and how the writer felt about them.

Listen to the poem read aloud to you.

Looking into the box

1 After hearing the poem read once or twice, jot down your own responses to the following:
   - How do you think the writer feels about the gift?
   - How does she use it?
   - What do you think the golden tree is in the poem?
   - What are your favourite lines/phrases?
   - What scenes can you picture most vividly?

   Try completing the following statement:

   I think the poem is about…

   Share your original jottings with a partner or small group and see how closely you agree.

2 In a pair or individually, create your own collage of pictures from magazines, photographs, illustrations, material, or words/phrases to illustrate what the poem makes you see and understand. You may want to include key lines and phrases from the poem itself.

3 Create your own personal box by collecting eight to ten items that reflect your life, interests, hopes, and fears. Share this box with a partner, talking carefully about what each item represents. You could include material, letters, photographs, clothes, keepsakes, books, music.

My box is made of golden oak,
my lover's gift to me.
He fitted hinges and a lock
of brass and a bright key.
He made it out of winter nights,
sanded and oiled and planed,
engraved inside the heavy lid
in brass, a golden tree.

In my box are twelve black books
where I have written down
how we have sanded, oiled and planed,
planted a garden, built a wall,
seen jays and goldcrests, rare red kites,
found the wild heartsease, drilled a well,
harvested apples and words and days
and planted a golden tree.

On an open shelf I keep my box.
Its key is in the lock.
I leave it there for you to read,
or them, when we are dead,
how everything is slowly made,
how slowly things made me,
a tree, a lover, words, a box,
books and a golden tree.

Gillian Clarke

46

Another Box

Before you look at the poem below, brainstorm the story of
Pandora's Box and see if, as a class, you can re-tell the story.
Then, with this in mind, listen to the poem below.

I will put in the box

the swish of a silk sari on a summer night,
fire from the nostrils of a Chinese dragon,
the tip of a tongue touching a tooth.

I will put in the box

a snowman with a rumbling belly,
a sip of the bluest water from Lake Lucerne,
a leaping spark from an electric fish.

I will put in the box

three violet wishes spoken in Gujarati,
the last joke of an ancient uncle
and the first smile of a baby.

I will put in the box

a fifth season and a black sun,
a cowboy on a broomstick
and a witch on a white horse.

My box is fashioned from ice and gold and
    steel,
with stars on the lid and secrets in the
    corners.
Its hinges are the toe joints
of dinosaurs.

I shall surf in my box
on the great high-rolling breakers of the wild
    Atlantic,
then wash ashore on a yellow beach
the colour of the sun.

Kit Wright

Comparisons

1 As a class, discuss:
   ■ how Kit Wright feels about the
     contents of his box
   ■ how the contents of this box differ
     from those in Pandora's Box
2 Use Kit Wright's poem as a model and
  write your own list poem about 'The
  Magic Box', describing a box and what
  you would put in it.

Taking it further

You will have noticed that the titles of the
poems by Gillian Clarke and Kit Wright have
been removed. In your pairs, decide on a
title for each poem and be prepared to
justify your choice to the class.

Ballads

Another favourite way of telling stories in verse is to use ballad form. Ballads first were told in the Middle Ages to record valiant deeds, family feuds, and tragic love stories. They often contained dialogue and told the story in vivid key scenes.

In a pair, share the following gruesome Australian ballad that tells of a terrible wedding night.

The Griesly Wife

'Lie still, my newly married wife,
    Lie easy as you can.
You're young and ill accustomed yet
    To sleeping with a man.'

The snow lay thick, the moon was full
    And shone across the floor.
The young wife went with never a word
    Barefooted to the door.

He up and followed sure and fast,
    The moon shone clear and white.
But before his coat was on his back
    His wife was out of sight.

He trod the trail wherever it turned
    By many a mound and scree,
And still the barefoot track led on
    And an angry man was he.

He followed fast, he followed slow,
    And still he called her name,
But only the dingoes of the hills
    Yowled back at him again.

His hair stood up along his neck,
    His angry mind was gone,
For the track of the two bare feet gave out
    And a four-foot track went on.

Her nightgown lay upon the snow
    As it might upon the sheet,
But the track that led on from where it lay
    Was never of human feet.

His heart turned over in his chest,
    He looked from side to side,
And he thought more of his gumwood fire
    Than he did of his griesly bride.

At first he started walking back
    And then began to run
And his quarry wheeled at the end of her track
    And hunted him in turn.

Oh, long the fire may burn for him
    And open stand the door,
And long the bed may wait empty:
    He'll not be back any more.

John Manifold

Thinking about the poem

1 In your own words try re-telling the story to each other, explaining what happened verse by verse.

2 Now try and devise a ballad recipe.

- What incident and action might you have?
- What is the rhyme pattern in each verse?
- How many strong beats do you get in each line?

Using your ideas, report back to the class to compile a full recipe which can either go on the board or into your books to help you with the next assignment.

Lord Ullin's Daughter

The next ballad, which appears on page 50, has been printed out of sequence. See if you can recreate the story of *Lord Ullin's Daughter* by rearranging the verses. The first two verses and the last two are in the right order. By careful reading and by working in a group of four see if you can agree on the correct order of the rest.

Before you begin, look back at your ballad recipe, and see if you have included the following points:

- a ballad tells a story with a setting and action
- a verse has four lines
- verses have a rhyme scheme of a b c b
- ballads have verses with a regular rhythm, usually with a beat of 4 3 4 3 or 4 4 4 4 in each verse

Does *Lord Ullin's Daughter* follow this pattern?

Performing the poem

Having decided on a final order for the poem, prepare a rehearsed performance of the ballad that can either be taped or produced for the rest of the class. Use different voices for each of the characters and remember to include a narrator. First mark your text so each person's lines are clear and then decide on the tone, volume and pace of the reading. Practise your reading several times before your final attempt.

Lord Ullin's Daughter

1
A chieftain, to the Highlands bound,
    Cries, 'Boatman, do not tarry,
And I'll give thee a silver pound
    To row us o'er the ferry.'

2
'Now who be ye would cross Lochgyle,
    This dark and stormy water?'
'O, I'm the chief of Ulva's isle,
    And this Lord Ullin's daughter.

3
And still they rowed amidst the roar
    Of waters fast prevailing;
Lord Ullin reached that fatal shore,
    His wrath was changed to wailing.

4
The boat has left a stormy land,
    A stormy sea before her –
When, oh! too strong, for human hand,
    The tempest gathered o'er her.

5
'O haste thee, haste!' the lady cries,
    'Though tempests round us gather;
I'll meet the raging of the skies,
    But not an angry father.'

6
But still as wilder blew the wind,
    And as the night grew drearer,
Adown the glen rode armed men,
    Their trampling sounded nearer.

7
'And by my word! the bonny bird
    In danger shall not tarry;
So though the waves are raging white,
    I'll row you o'er the ferry.'

8
For sore dismayed, through storm and shade,
    His child he did discover:
One lovely hand she stretched for aid,
    And one was round her lover.

9
Out spoke the hardy Highland wight,
    'I'll go, my chief, I'm ready!
It is not for your silver bright;
    But for your winsome lady.

10
'His horsemen hard behind us ride;
    Should they our steps discover,
Then who will cheer my bonny bride
    When they have slain her lover?'

11
By this the storm grew loud apace,
    The water-wraith was shrieking,
And in the scowl of Heaven each face
    Grew dark as they were speaking.

12
'And fast before her father's men
    Three days we've fled together,
For should he find us in the glen,
    My blood would stain the heather.

13
'Come back! come back!' he cried in grief,
    'Across this stormy water;
And I'll forgive your Highland chief,
    My daughter! Oh, my daughter!'

14
'Twas vain: the loud waves lashed the shore,
    Return or aid preventing;
The waters wild went o'er his child,
    And he was left lamenting.

Thomas Campbell

Taking it further

There is a lot of this poem that is left unexplained. For example, we are not told why the father disapproves of his daughter's choice or how the couple escaped.

1 As a group, make a list of questions that you could ask so that the 'untold' parts of the story become clearer. Then together decide what you think happened before and after the events in the poem. After your performance of the ballad, your group will take on the role of the father and will answer any questions posed by your audience. Any member of the group may answer but you must ensure you have agreed your story. If an unexpected question comes up, listen carefully to whatever answer is given so you do not contradict it when you answer later questions.

2 Following the role play, take the part of the father and write a journal entry for a month after the incident, relating:
- what happened before the chase
- his feelings
- the pursuit and drowning
- later incidents
- whether he would change events

The father's request is that this 'journal' is buried with the bodies of the daughter and her lover.

Poem as Picture
Reflecting on Pictures

Have you ever found yourself staring deep into a Magic Image picture, only to step back startled as a landscape suddenly appears in front of you?

The same happens in the following poems. As the writers look at reflections, suddenly a different, totally unexpected image appears, which was there all the time.

On your own, read the Judith Nicholls poem below.

Magic Mirror

*Step before the magic mirror,
tell me what you see?*

Could it be
    me, stretched tall,
    unfolded, gaudy blanket,
    giant transfer
    ironed to the wall,
    a sprawl of paint
    splashed in a dull hall
    by a lonely stair?

Could it be
    some painted circus clown
    blown from a nearby town,
    oil, marbled in a puddle,
    fuddled stained-glass window,
    Joseph's coloured coat,
    or splintered light
    from Noah's rainbow,
    low in a torn grey sky,
    after the storm?

Could it be
    Christmas crackers
    in wrappers tinselled
    and bright as a glass bauble,
    a summer garden
    dancing through rainy glass,
    waving flags, each one
    flown for a fair princess,
    or trembling wings
    of dragonflies,
    caught in August sun?

You look in the magic mirror,
tell me what you see;
is that really only – me?

Judith Nicholls

Responding to the poem

Complete these statements with your own ideas:

■ I think this poem is about …
■ The scenes I can picture most vividly are …
■ My favourite lines/phrases are …

Share your observations with a friend, explaining why you made the choices you did and comparing these choices.

Magic mirror images

Using the illustration to help you, write down what you see in the mirror. (It may help to squint so the image contorts even more.) When you have four or five ideas, share these in a group of four. Your group can then share the best ideas with the class to construct three more verses for the poem.

More pictures

It isn't just distorted mirrors that throw back odd pictures. Any reflection can appear very unusual if you look at it carefully.

1 Begin by brainstorming all the places where you might find a reflection. Here are some to get you started:

- a puddle
- a polished surface
- a Christmas tree ball
- a T.V. screen
- the glass of a display case

2 Read the following poems through carefully. Titles and lines that give clues as to what is creating the reflection, and where, have been removed and put at the bottom of the page. Match the missing lines with the right poem and note down the lines/images you like the most.

A
Long buildings hang and
wriggle gently. Chimneys
are bent legs bouncing
on clouds below. A flag
wags like a fishhook
down there in the sky.

The arched stone bridge
is an eye, with underlid
in the water. In its lens
dip crinkled heads with hats
that don't fall off. Dogs go by,
barking on their backs.
A baby, taken to feed the
duck, dangles upside-down,
a pink balloon for a buoy.

Treetops deploy a haze of
cherry bloom for roots,
where birds coast belly-up
in the glass bowl of a hill;
from its bottom a bunch
of peanut-munching children
is suspended by their
sneakers, waveringly.

A swan, with twin necks
forming the figure three,
steers between two dimpled
towers doubled. Fondly
hissing, she kisses herself,
and all the scene is troubled:
water-windows splinter,
tree-limbs tangle, the bridge
folds like a fan.

May Swenson

B
Looking up and
up and up to
me gives him
a funny feeling:
Why do grown-
up mirrors
need to show
such a lot
of ceiling?

Philip Gross

C
I show
him his face
very small and alone
in the dark. Is that what
makes him throw
a stone?

Philip Gross

D

You're only as old
as you feel, me lad,
eh?
He's attempting
to straighten
his tie
and his moustache. (I
don't reply.)
There's life
in the old
dog yet…
But he can't
look himself in the eye.

Philip Gross

1 A deep well looks back at a boy
2 Toddler at his parents' mirror
3 Water picture
4 In the pond in the park
all things are double:
5 Drunken uncle in the Gents at the
Bodger's Arms

Writing your own

1 Look again at the list you made of places
where you might see a reflection. Choose
one of these and think carefully about
just what you see.
2 Now, although your picture may seem
very bizarre, write down just what you see.
Try to look at each level, the surface, the
reflection and what is in the surface
(e.g. glass case, reflection, contents of
case). Use the ideas in the poems above
to help you.

From Another Angle – Riddles

1 The photographs on these pages are of very ordinary everyday objects, taken from unusual angles. In a pair, see if you can identify what they are and decide what gave you the clues.

2 Riddles are similar puzzles: they use words to describe objects in unusual ways. On this page are eight riddles. By reading carefully, see if you can identify what they are. (If you get stuck, the answers are at the end of this section.) Again, in your pair discuss the lines that gave you the clues.

A

The ghost of all our rubbish come to haunt us.
A ragged crow that blows about the garden.
A giant's burnt rice pudding skin.
Black ice waiting to be skidded on.
The shroud of many unimportant things.
A limbless, bulging belly.
A cauldron brewing garbage soup.
A witch's plastic mac.
The envelope for a long black letter.
The silent hungry beggar at my door.

Sue Cowling

B

        Riddle my this, riddle my that –
          guess my riddle or perhaps not.
Eyes ablaze looking up,
Four-Legs crouch near Four-Legs –
what is it?

James Berry

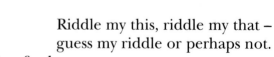

C

        Riddle my this, riddle my that –
          guess my riddle or perhaps not.
Waltzing for leaves
waltzing on grass
and put back to stand in corner –
what is it?

James Berry

▼ **D**

Though not a cow
I have horns;
Though not an ass
I carry a pack-saddle;
And wherever I go
I leave silver behind me.

Trad.

▼ **E**

I am a see-through pear
Hanging from my treeless branch.
A bit of a conjuror I can ripen suddenly,
Or disappear at a switch.
Like the apple I am good for you
Lengthening your days.

John Cotton

▼ **F**

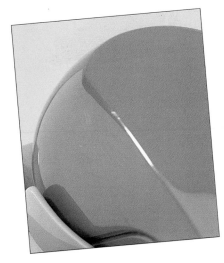

I am the shame beneath a carpet.
No one comes to sweep me off my feet.

Abandoned rooms and unread books collect me.
Sometimes I dance like particles of light.

My legions thicken on each windowpane,
A gathering of dusk, perpetual gloom,

And when at last the house has fallen,
I am the cloud left hanging in the air.

John Mole

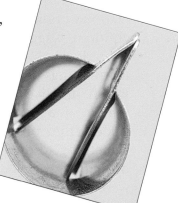

▼ **G**

I am an instrument, a pipe,
A bright brass concertina
Making heavenly music.
Planets, spheres, the Plough, the Milky Way
All come at my calling
Winking at me, eye to eye,
As if they knew that he who plays me well
Will understand them, entering
The mystery of the universe and bringing closer
Infinite secrets held for aeons
In the darkness which I penetrate.

Play me in silence, and I'll give you
Silence in return
Though in your head, professor,
You'll be seeing stars.

John Mole

▼ **H**

Grand and solo, polished brightly,
Dance of practised fingers nightly,
Clair-de-lunar or moonlightly.

Presto, forte, pathetique,
The world is mine because I speak
A language common yet unique.

I tax to brilliant extremes
Each maestro's formalistic dreams,
All variations and all themes.

Then, when his energy withdraws
To where you sit amazed, I pause
And share with him in the applause.

John Mole

57

Gillian Clarke on metaphor

A riddle works by describing one thing as though it is something else: it uses metaphors. Below, the poet Gillian Clarke describes working with a class, where creating metaphors and similes seemed to happen almost by accident. Read the article through by yourself.

Sometimes to help children to make really surprising images, I play a trick on them. First I ask them to suggest subjects for poems. In Llannon Primary School, Dyfed, the children suggested 'The Spider'. Then I asked them to tell me as many things as they could think of which are like the spider. I said, 'Think of a person who is like a spider. Think of a machine. Think of something to do with the weather, or nature, or your house.' There were many good ideas, like acrobat, architect, builder, electric whisk, sewing machine, knitting needles, God, the moon, a snowflake. Any of them would do but I chose acrobat.

Next I wrote down 'The Acrobat' on a new piece of paper. Secretly I remembered that the children had told me the acrobat is like a spider. The children thought of all the things they could say about an acrobat. I wrote it all down. When the page was full, the poem was ready. I crossed out the word 'acrobat' and wrote 'The Spider' as the new title. That was the trick.

They were very surprised, as they had thought their poem would be called 'The Acrobat'. Here it is.

The Spider

Daring and skilful,
determined to dazzle
he performs his tricks on the rope,
turns cartwheels on his wire.

He rides his delicate bicycle
wheels spinning
a tumble-drier
a whirlwind.

He perfects his tricks
walks on stilts on wire
It shines like silver
strong as gold.

He balances to music
drums beating
as he walks on his hands.

Do you think the trick worked? I do.
It is exciting to think of the spider
doing all those things in his shining
morning web, just like an acrobat.

Gillian Clarke

Writing your own

Now using Gillian Clarke's method, as a class try writing your own riddle.

1 For a first try, take something like a snail. Write down all the things you can think of which are like the snail.
   - If the snail was a person with a job, what would it be?
   - If it was a craft, what would it be?
   - If it was a household appliance, what would it be?
   - A colour?
   - A weather?
   - A food?
   - An item of clothing?

2 Now choose one of these ideas to work on in particular, although other details can be slipped into your poem too. Take this idea and write down all the things you can say about it.

3 Once all the ideas are on the board, split into pairs and rearrange those ideas into a riddle, missing off the title so that other readers would have to guess what it was about. After fifteen minutes share your pieces and decide on favourites.

4 Finally, either in a pair or individually, use the same technique to write your own riddles. As you are writing, remember that you are comparing one thing to another to help your reader picture it more clearly. By saying one thing is something else, you are using a metaphor. You may find that you want to compare something to a person: this technique, which we call personification, can be very effective. You will find more about this in the next section.

Gillian Clarke

Answers

A A dustbin liner
B A dog begging at a table
C A garden broom for sweeping leaves
D A snail
E A light bulb
F Dust
G A telescope
H A piano

Personification

In the two poems below, Forest and the Sun are described as though they are very different women. Describing an object as though it is a person is called personification.

The best words in the best places

The poet has used particular adjectives, nouns, and verbs in each poem to give an idea of the kind of women Forest and Sun are. Some of these have been taken out, muddled, and put in a box opposite. Using clues from the poem, and what you consider to be the best words in the best places, rewrite the poems, discussing your choices with your partner.

For Forest

Forest could keep secrets
Forest could keep secrets

Forest _____ in every day
to watersound and birdsound
Forest letting her hair down
to the teeming creeping of her forest-ground

But Forest don't _____ her business
no Forest cover her business down
from sky and fast-eye sun
and when night come
and darkness _____ her like a _____
Forest is a bad dream woman.

Forest _____ about mountain
and when earth was young
Forest dreaming of the _____ of gold
Forest roosting with mysterious eldorado

and when howler monkey
wake her up with howl
Forest just _____ and _____
to a new day of sound

but coming back to secrets
Forest could keep secrets
Forest could keep secrets
    And we must keep Forest.

Grace Nichols

Sun is Laughing

This morning she got up
on the ____ side of bed,
pulled back
the grey sky-curtains
and ____ her head
through the blue window
of heaven,
her ____ laughter
____ over,
falling broad across the grass,
____ the washing on the line,
giving more shine
to the back of a ladybug
and ____ up all the world.

Then, without any warning,
as if she was suddenly ____,
or just got ____
because she could hear no one
giving praise
to her ____ ways,
Sun ____ the sky-window close,
plunging the whole world
into greyness once more.

O Sun, ____ one,
how can we live
without the ____ of your face?

Grace Nichols

stretch	wrap
happy	brightening
gown	broadcast
yellow	sulky
poked	spilling
tune	shining
moody	dreaming
stir	holiday
bored	slammed
caress	buttering

Taking it further

1 In your pair, discuss the kind of woman described in each poem. What clothes would she wear? What job might she do? Where would she live? Describe her room, her moods. What kind of age would she be? What about her family and friends?

2 On your own, describe either Forest or Sun as though they were this woman, using the ideas above. Begin: 'She is … ' Be prepared to explain what lines in the poem made you think of her like this.

3 Share your ideas with a group of four. After you have heard each other's, prepare a reading of either *For Forest* or *Sun is Laughing*. Try to use your voices to convey the character of the person you see. (The notes on performing poems on page 73 will help you with this.)

Poem as Shape
Shaping Poems

One person's description of a particular event can take a number of different forms or shapes, and their ideas and pictures can be very different to other people's. In the next few pages, the focus will be on two festivals, Bonfire Night and birthdays, but you'll be expected to experiment with ideas to fit them into a variety of poetry forms.

Before considering the shape of a poem, it is important to think about its content. Poems can look at many aspects of a person, a place or an occurrence: the first poem on Bonfire Night was chosen because it looks beyond the excitement, colour, warmth, and parties, to the more sinister aspects of the whole event. When you begin your own writing you may want to return to these ideas.

Why?

Why do you turn your head, Suzanna,
And why do you swim your eye?
It's only the children of Bellman Street
Calling 'A Penny for the Guy!'

Why do you look away, Suzanna,
As the children wheel him by?
It's only a dummy in an old top-hat
And a fancy jacket and tie.

Why do you take my hand, Suzanna,
As the pointing flames jump high?
It's only a bundle of sacking and straw.
Nobody's going to die.

Why is your cheek so pale, Suzanna,
As the whizz bangs flash and fly?
It's nothing but a rummage of paper and rag
Strapped to a stick you spy.

Why do you say you hear, Suzanna,
The sound of a long, last sigh?
And why do you say it won't leave your head,
No matter how you try?

Best let me take you home, Suzanna,
Best on your bed to lie
It's only a dummy in an old top hat
Nobody's going to die.

Charles Causley

Questions about the poem

In a pair:
- decide why Suzanna is fearful
- write down any questions you would like to ask
- share your thoughts and ideas as a class

In contrast, the next two poems give a more celebratory view of fireworks themselves.

Fireworks

They rise like sudden fiery flowers
    That burst upon the night,
Then fall to earth in burning showers
    Of crimson, blue, and white.

Like buds too wonderful to name,
    Each miracle unfolds,
And catherine-wheels begin to flame
    Like whirling marigolds.

Rockets and Roman candles make
    An orchard of the sky,
Whence magic trees their petals shake
    Upon each gazing eye.

James Reeves

My Momentary Delights

My momentary delights
Are held close
In a paper bud.
I flower best at night,
My petals falling
Like bright showers
When I am fired to beauty.

John Cotton

Your own fireworks poems

You are now going to write your own fireworks poems, looking at how the shape of a poem gives it a particular impact.

1 Brainstorm

To start, brainstorm as a class all the words, phrases, and sentences you can think of to describe an aspect of firework night. You can 'borrow' phrases from the three poems above to get you started.

2 Fireworks verbs

In a pair, draw a firework base at the bottom of your page and write, coming from it, all the vivid verbs or doing words you can think of to describe flames and fireworks. You can use the ideas on the right to get you started. A thesaurus might help you in your final stages.

unfolding, palpitating, shivering, whirling, bursting, showering, gobbling, bubbling, arching

3 Describing fireworks

Still in your pairs, choose fourteen words to describe a firework to someone who has never seen one before. You can use phrases or words from the poems above but try to be original. See if you can include at least one contrast or comparison that springs to mind when you think of fireworks. Remember – no more than fourteen words. Lay them out like the diagram on the right.

4 Diamante

Next, you are going to take your words and arrange them in a diamond pattern, which will describe one thing for half the poem and then another until the end of the poem. The best results come when you contrast two opposites in one poem like:

light/dark   fire/water
hot/cold   sorrow/joy

Continue to use your bonfire theme and see if you can lay it out like the piece below.

7 lines

Line 1	Noun 1	Darkness
Line 2	Adjective Adjective	Chill Predatory
Line 3	Verb + ing Verb + ing Verb + ing	Creeping Stealing Hiding
Line 4	Synonym synonym / Stark contrast / Synonym synonym	Bereaver Hunter. Entertainer acrobat
Line 5	Verb + ing Verb + ing Verb + ing	Juggling Giggling Beaming
Line 6	Adjective Adjective	Heated Fiery
Line 7	Noun 2	Firework

5 Syllable poems

Now break your words into syllables to produce a 'growing poem'. Here, lines grow as the piece progresses, from one syllable in the first line to five in the last.

As you write all the next poems, try and include a comparison in your word picture as well as counting the syllables.

Look
I see
the condemned
grasping at the
grim flames in terror

Anne Powling

Guy,
bundle
of paper
a wilting rag-
doll in greedy flames

Anne Powling

6 Haiku
Next try and develop your 'growing poems' into Haiku.
First read the following haiku by Gina Douthwaite.

Haiku

Tantrums of flame gush
from throats of gunpowder tubes.
Take notice of me!

Bones of bonfire shift.
Startled sparks light up skull-eyed
faces in bushes.

Wisp of grey veil floats,
like some weary Guy Fawkes' ghost,
out through night's black walls.

Spent sparklers spear out
in webs of wire weaponry
at anxious ankles.

High over midnight
an insistent arc of stars,
still stage-struck, signs off.

Gina Douthwaite

In a haiku you are expected to suggest a lot
in just a few words. You have three lines:

> Line 1 has five syllables
> Line 2 has seven syllables
> Line 3 has five syllables

There is no rhyme but there is usually an
image or picture suggesting a particular
feeling or mood. For example, the third
haiku, comparing the smoke to a ghost, gives
the reader a taste of the sinister aspects of
Bonfire Night, just from the one picture.

Working in a pair or individually, try to write
three or four haiku.

Taking it further

When you have finished, take one example
from each of your sections. Write them up on
one piece of paper and illustrate your work
either with collage or with your own
illustration.

Verse Pictures

Patterns in poems are not always as tightly structured as the ones above. The poet often decides to split each poem into separate sections called verses.

Building a picture

In the next two poems, each verse gives you a better picture of the person being described. The titles of both poems have been removed. Listen to the two pieces read aloud and then on your own, answer the following questions:

1 Who is Billy?
2 How does what we know about the character in each poem change from verse to verse?
3 Complete the statement: I think the poems are about …
4 Decide on a title for each one.
5 Complete the idea: For me, the differences between the two poems are that …

As you finish, share your ideas with a partner. How far are your observations similar?

When I was six
Everyone had birthday parties.
We always had Dead Lions,
Musical Bumps, Being Sick
And Pass the Parcel…

Between each wrapper
Round the swollen present
Lay tucked a toffee
Or a lollipop –
And everybody got a turn
At taking off a layer.

When I was nine, I learned
That the way the music stopped
Was not by chance:
My father's gaze took in
Each trembling lip, each face,
Each pair of hopeful eyes.

When I was twelve, I realized
With some surprise
That later on in life
There's no one there
To press the switch
And make sure
That everything is fair
And everybody
Gets their
Share.

Trevor Millum

66

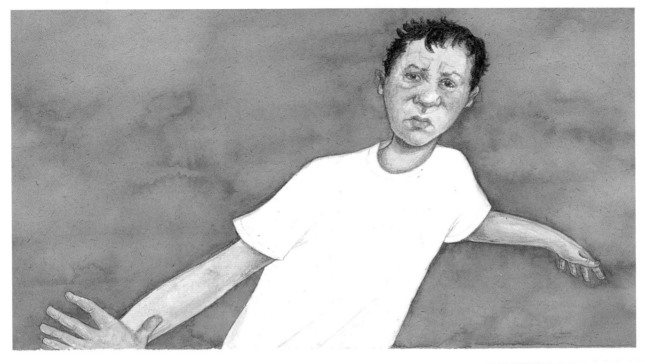

I know a lad called Billy
Who goes along with me
He plays this game
Where he uses my name
And makes people think that he's me.

Don't ever mess with Billy
He's a vicious sort of bloke
He'll give you a clout
For saying nowt
And thump you for a joke.

My family can't stand Billy
Can't bear him round the place
He won't eat his food
He's rough and rude
And wears scowls all over his face.

No one can ever break Billy
He's got this look in his eye
That seems to say
You can wale me all day
But you'll not make Billy cry.

He has a crazy face has Billy
Eyes that look but can't see
A mouth like a latch
Ears that don't match
And a space where his brain should be.

Mad Billy left one morning
Crept away without being seen
Left his body for me
That fits perfectly
And a calm where his madness has been.

Gareth Owen

Writing your own

Trevor Millum's poem looks at the way our picture of the world
changes as we grow older. Try using the same verse pattern as
him to write your own piece about growing up. It could be
optimistic or pessimistic but each verse should begin:
When I was six ….
When I was nine, I learned …
When I was twelve, I realized …

Poem as Sound
Rhythm in Poetry

Use your feet to find the beat

Adrian Mitchell

Find the rhythm

Some poetry has such a strong rhythm that you can't help getting caught in the music and pace of the piece.

1 On your own, read the two poems below. In your head, find the rhythm of each one.

2 In groups of five, work on performing one of the poems. Choose your favourite out of the two and experiment with some of the following suggestions:

■ a beat box rhythm in the background
■ individual voices for some lines
■ group voices for some lines
■ perhaps one line or phrase repeated as a bass beat

It may be useful to make copies of the poem, so that your group can mark their parts on their copies in different colours, to show each person when to come in.

Rhythm

Rhythm rhythm
Can you
Hear the
Rhythm

If you listen close
Ears to the ground
The base of noise
Is rhythm's sound
From spoken words
To ways of walk
From rapping to reggae
And funk we talk in

Rhythm rhythm
Can you
Hear the
Rhythm

Way back in the heart of Africa
They took our drums away
But rhythm proved its own power
By being here today

All four corners
Sweet sounding Rhythms reach
With treble in the speakers
And bass in the speech
From the depths of cold
To heat in heights
Mohammid Ali did do it in fights

With
Quick Rhythms
Slick Rhythms
Bold Rhythms
Gold Rhythms
God given
Rhythm Rhythm
Can you
hear the
Rhythm Rhythm

Rhythm Rhythm
Can you
hear the
Rhythm

Lemn Sissay

Vegan Delight

Ackees, chapatties
Dumplins an nan,
Channa an rotis
Onion uttapam,
Masala dosa
Green callaloo
Bhel an samosa
Corn an aloo.
Yam an cassava
Pepperpot stew,
Rotlo an guava
Rice an tofu,
Puri, paratha
Sesame casserole,
Brown eggless pasta
An brown bread rolls.

Soya milked muesli
Soya bean curd,
Soya sweet sweeties
Soya's de word,
Soya bean margarine
Soya bean sauce,
What can mek medicine?
Soya of course.
Soya meks yoghurt
Soya ice-cream,
Or soya sorbet
Soya reigns supreme,
Soya sticks liquoriced
Soya salads
Try any soya dish
Soya is bad.

Plantain an tabouli
Cornmeal pudding
Onion bhajee
Wid plenty cumin,
Breadfruit an coconuts
Molasses tea
Dairy free omelettes
Very chilli.
Ginger bread, nut roast
Sorrell, paw paw,
Cocoa an rye toast
I tek dem on tour,
Drinking cool maubi
Meks me feel sweet,
What was dat question now?
What do we eat?

Benjamin Zephaniah

Taking it further

1 Share your own 'rap' favourites from past or present chart music and try performing some so the class can share it.

2 Discuss the kind of subjects that come up in raps and why you think this is.

3 Now watch the video clip of Benjamin Zephaniah performing *Vegan Delight* and answering questions from students. As you watch, note down:
 ■ where he gets his ideas from – what sorts of subjects are his raps about?
 ■ the sort of language he uses when writing raps

■ how he gets started
■ how he uses a chorus
■ why he thinks raps are so popular

Using these ideas, work in a group of five to produce your own rap on a subject of your own choice. If you get stuck, you may want to try one in Benjamin Zephaniah's style about favourite food, or use Lemn Sissay's chorus and write about different rhythms that occur around you, like waves, clocks, your heartbeat, etc.

Onomatopoeia

Words and phrases can do more than move to a rhythm. Many words can talk back at you, their sounds reminding you of what they mean, like *squelch*, *chatter*, and *slop*. Words like these are examples of onomatopoeia.

Mimicking meaning

In a pair, read the Judith Nicholls poem below. Not only does she find alternative words for *said*, but many of the words she chooses mimic the sound of their meaning, like *murmur*. Together, pick the ones that work best for you, reminding you of the noise described.

Your own walking words

1 Now, as a class, brainstorm all the words you could use instead of *to go*. You could start with *amble*, *tiptoe*, *tap*, *trample* …

2 When you have forty or more, in pairs try writing your own version of the piece below, calling it 'Teacher Goes'. Don't worry if you can't make your poem rhyme – the most important thing is to enjoy playing with the words.

Teacher Said…

You can use
    mumbled and muttered,
    groaned, grumbled and uttered,
    professed, droned or stuttered
        … but *don't* use SAID!

You can use
    rant or recite,
    yell, yodel or snort,
    bellow, murmur or moan,
    you can grunt or just groan
        … but *don't* use SAID!

You can
    hum, howl and hail,
    scream, screech, shriek or bawl,
    squeak, snivel or squeal
    with a blood-curdling wail
        … but *don't* use SAID!

        … SAID my teacher.

Judith Nicholls

70

Sound Echoes Sense

When a poem is read aloud, the listener can get a much clearer understanding of the piece from:
- the sound of various phrases
- the emphasis given by similar sounds
- the tone of voice
- the volume and the pace of the reading

Machines

Before you work with the 'noise' poems that follow, try and think about how you can produce soothing sounds and disruptive, explosive noise as you try the following activity.

Divide yourselves into groups of six. One group will work at a time.

Cold Comfort

1 One person in the group moves into a space and begins a machine-like movement and noise. The next person should watch, think, and then join in the activity, adding another part to the machine. This can be done by linking in some way to the action of any people already in the machine. Try and develop:
  - a car assembly line, beating, cutting and fitting door panels to a car
  - a baby's incubator, including the baby's breathing

There should be no communication within groups before the activity begins. Later groups can build on the ideas of earlier groups.

2 Each group is given a picture of one of two Heath Robinson machines. The groups must use sound alone to mimic the working of the machine in front of them, as it goes from stage to stage. Remember:
  - more than one person could make a particular noise
  - think about the speed of each stage
  - the people who start the process do not necessarily stop when the next stage starts
  - think carefully about volume

Your audience should be able to recognize the sounds that mimic each stage by looking at their diagrams and listening to you.

Ending in Smoke

Poems in performance

The aim now is to take what you have learnt from your quiet and noisy sound collages, and use the ideas to help create a choral reading of one of the following poems.

Nightride

The road unwinding under our wheels
New in the headlamps like a roll of foil.
The rain is a recorder writing tunes
In telegraph wires, kerbs and cats' eyes,
Reflections and the lights of little towns.

He turns his head to look at me.
'Why are you quiet?' Shiny road rhythm,
Rain rhythm, beat of the windscreen wipers,
I push my knee against his in the warmth
And the car thrusts the dark and rain away.

The child sleeps, and I reflect, as I breathe
His brown hair, and watch the apple they gave him
Held in his hot hands, that a tree must ache
With the sweet weight of the round rosy fruit,
As I with Dylan's head, nodding on its stalk.

Gillian Clarke

Blacksmiths

Swarthy smoke-blackened smiths, smudged with soot,
Drive me to death with the din of their banging.
Men never knew such a noise at night!
Such clattering and clanging, such clamour of scoundrels!
Crabbed and crooked, they cry, 'Coal! Coal!'
And blow with their bellows till their brains burst.
'Huff! Puff!' pants one: 'Haff! Paff!' another.
They spit and they sprawl and they spin many yarns.
They grate and grind their teeth, and groan together,
Hot with the heaving of their hard hammers.
Aprons they have, of hide of the bull,
And greaves as leg-guards against glowing sparks.
Heavy hammers they have, and hit hard with them;
Sturdy strokes they strike on their steel anvils.
Lus, bus! Las, bas! they beat in turn –
Such a doleful din, may the Devil destroy it!
The smith stretches a scrap, strikes a smaller,
Twines the two together, and tinkles a treble note:
Tik, tak! Hic, hac! Tiket, taket! Tyk, tak!
Bus, lus! Bas, las! Such a life they lead,
These Dobbin-dressers: Christ doom them to misery!
There's no rest at night from the noise of their water-fizzing.

Anon. Middle English, translated by Brian Stone

Performing the poems

In groups of five, prepare a rehearsed reading of your chosen piece. The aim is to bring the scene to life, in all its chaotic noise or tranquil serenity.

Begin by ensuring that each person has their own copy of the poem. Then, as a group, read the piece through and discuss the following questions.

1 How many voices will you have at various points?

2 Will you repeat or echo any lines or phrases? You might want to do this like a round in music.

3 Will any sounds continue as a bass line through the piece?

4 Will you vary the tone of voice for different lines?

5 Which words and sounds will you emphasize?

6 Where you will go fast and slow?

7 Which parts will be loud or soft?

8 Will you create any sound effects, e.g. rain on a car roof?

9 Will you position readers at different points around the room during performance?

Take time to rehearse your piece thoroughly and ask for advice from your listeners.

When you perform your piece, contrast the noisy poem with the quiet one, and enjoy the effect.

Alliteration

In *Blacksmiths*, the poet has created an explosive sound by beginning words in the same line with the same letter,

e.g. <u>b</u>low their <u>b</u>ellows till their <u>b</u>rains <u>b</u>urst.

Here the 'b' sounds echo the huff and puff of the hard work. This technique is called alliteration and was used a great deal in early English writing.

Alliteration is used in the extract opposite from the Anglo-Saxon poem *Beowulf*. A terrible monster, Grendel, has been terrorizing a settlement, murdering the warriors as they sleep. Beowulf has sworn he will fight this monster, so he lies in wait in the Great Hall for the beast to arrive. He watches as Grendel kills one of his warriors, then he strides forward to fight.

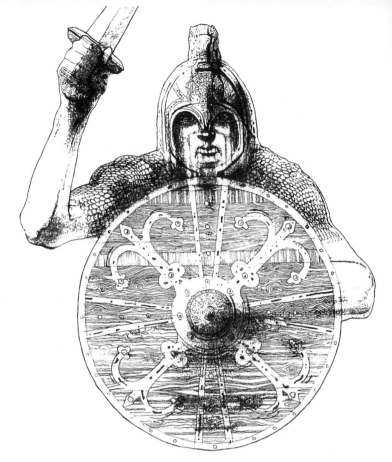

Rewriting the battle

1 Read the story of the conflict. Then, as a class, brainstorm as many verbs and adjectives as you can to show the noise, chaos, pain, and horror of the fight, and the anger of the two fighters.

2 When you have got as many words as you can think of, try arranging them in alphabetical order. Look for odd combinations that work well in sound or sense to convey the fight.

3 In a pair, use these word clusters to rewrite the extract. Use alliteration and onomatopoeia to bring the noisy scene to life.

4 When you have finished, decide who will read the piece out, rehearse this reading, and share your battle-scenes as a class.

Beowulf on video

Once you have read your own accounts aloud, watch the performance on video of an extract from the original Anglo-Saxon version of *Beowulf*. You will not be able to understand all of the words, but you can listen for the way the original author has used alliteration.

Now watch the piece again. Use the transcript from the Teacher's Book to help you note down:
■ which phrases you like the best and why
■ any words you recognize
Share these as a class.

Beowulf

Grendel slobbered spittle and blood; his first taste of flesh only made him more ravenous. He wheeled round towards Beowulf, stooped, reached out for him, and Beowulf…

Beowulf leaped up and stayed the monster's outstretched arm.

Grendel grunted and pulled back. And at that sound, all the other Geats were instantly awake. They grabbed their swords, they backed off, they shouted for Beowulf.

Grendel tried to break free but Beowulf held him fast. The monster snorted and tugged, he could feel his fingers cracking in the Geat's grip.

Now the great room boomed. Clang and clatter shattered the night-silence as Beowulf and Grendel lurched to and fro in their deathly tug-of-war. Tables and mead-benches were overturned, Grendel roared and snarled, and in the outbuildings Danes woke and listened in the darkness.

When the Geats saw that Grendel could not escape Beowulf's grip, they surrounded him and slashed at him with their swords.

Heorot flashed with battle-lights. Those warriors did not know that no kind of weapon, not even the finest iron on earth, could wound their enemy. His skin was like old rind, tough and almost hard; he had woven a secret spell against every kind of battle-blade.

Now Beowulf twisted Grendel's right arm behind his neck. He locked it and turned it, slowly he turned it, putting terrible pressure on Grendel's shoulder.

The monster bellowed and dropped to one knee. He jerked and his whole body shuddered and trembled. With superhuman strength he jerked again as he tried to escape Beowulf's grip, he jerked and all at once, his right shoulder ripped. A ghastly tearing of muscle and sinew and flesh; a spurting of hot blood: the monster's arm came apart from his body. Grendel howled. He staggered away from Beowulf, and reeled out of the hall.

Anon. Anglo-Saxon, translated by Kevin Crossley-Holland

75

Language Study
Verbs of Doing and Being

Verbs are often called 'doing words', because they are the class of words which supply the *action* of a sentence. But, as you learned in Book 1, many verbs are actually 'being' words, and are not really about actions at all.

'The Griesly Wife'

There are some examples of the different uses of 'doing' and 'being' verbs in the ballad of *The Griesly Wife* on page 48.

The story begins with six lines of verbs which don't involve much 'action' at all:

> 'Lie still, my newly married wife,
>   Lie easy as you can.
> You're young and ill accustomed yet
>   To sleeping with a man.'
>
> The snow lay thick, the moon was full
>   And shone across the floor.

This is because the poet is setting the scene, telling us how things *were*, rather than what the characters or things *did*.

The actions begin on line 7 and build up through the rest of the ballad, as we can see from the poet's use of action verbs from verse 4 onwards:

> He trod the trail wherever it turned
>   By many a mound and scree…

Pick out the action verbs from verses 5 and 6.

In verse 7, the poet uses mainly non-action verbs, as there is a pause in the action when the man stands looking at the nightgown in the snow:

> Her nightgown lay upon the snow
>   As it might upon the sheet,
> But the track that led on from where it lay
>   Was never of human feet.

Finally, pick out the action verbs from verse 9, when the frightened man turns for home, and the being verbs in the final two lines, which describe the empty house.

'Fireworks'

Pick out the verbs in the poem Fireworks on page 63.

Why do you think there are only action verbs in this poem, and no being verbs?

'When I was six...'

Trevor Millum's poem on page 66 contains a mixture of action verbs and being verbs.

Which two being verbs are important in showing how the speaker comes to understand things as he or she grows up?

Beowulf and Grendel

As you would expect, the account of the fight between Beowulf and Grendel on page 75 is packed with action verbs.

In pairs, look at the two extracts printed here, which have had some of the action verbs removed. Don't struggle to recall what they were, but decide on action verbs which will fit the story. Choose verbs as interesting and exciting as you can.

...The monster _____ed and _____ed, he could feel his fingers _____ing in the Geat's grip.

Now the great room ____ed. Clang and clatter _____ed the night-silence as Beowulf and Grendel _____ed to and fro in their deathly tug-of-war. Tables and mead-benches were _____ed, Grendel ____ed and ____ed, and in the outbuildings Danes woke and listened in the darkness.

When the Geats saw that Grendel could not escape Beowulf's grip, they _____ed him and _____ed at him with their swords...

...Now Beowulf _____ed Grendel's right arm behind his neck. He _____ed it and ____ed it, slowly he _____ed it, putting terrible pressure on Grendel's shoulder.

The monster ____ed and dropped to one knee. He _____ed and his whole body _____ed and _____ed...

Synonyms

The poem *Teacher Said…* on page 70 is largely made up of words which can all take the place of 'said'.

Words which have roughly the same meaning are known as 'synonyms' (from two Ancient Greek words meaning 'same' and 'name'). For example, we might say that 'large' and 'big' are synonyms; or 'happy', 'merry', and 'cheerful'.

Synonyms are useful because they give us a variety of words to choose from and also help us if we do not want to repeat words. For example, phrases including the word 'get' can be over-used in speech and writing. Which synonyms (or near synonyms) could replace 'get' phrases in the following passage? (In most cases one word can replace two. For example, 'I got out of…' can become 'I left…')

You might find it helpful to use a thesaurus (see the opposite page).

I got the washing up done, got my coat on, got out of the house as quickly as I could and got to the bus-stop by six o'clock. I got really cold waiting, but finally got the six-thirty and got to town by seven. I got Charlie to get me a burger and had got over my stomach upset by the time we had got into the cinema. It was pretty full and we nearly didn't get seats. The film was in French and I didn't get the jokes at first but I got by in the end by reading the subtitles.

Nice work

1 In pairs, brainstorm all the expressions you can think of which might contain the word 'nice'. (For example, a nice meal, a nice day, a nice film…) Then find synonyms for each one. (An enjoyable meal, a pleasant day, an interesting film…)

2 Write a short passage like the one on the left, which contains about ten different examples of 'nice', and challenge another pair to provide synonyms. Compare their version with yours. Were there any words you hadn't thought of?

3 Finally, as a class, discuss how many different synonyms for 'nice' you have found.

Using a thesaurus

If you are trying to think of synonyms, or cannot quite find the right word to express a particular idea, or perhaps need examples of words which are all in the same area of meaning, you probably need a thesaurus. (The word comes from Ancient Greek and means a treasury or store-house.)

For example, on page 63 you were asked to think up all the vivid verbs to do with fireworks, and were offered some examples to start you off. Your job of thinking up related words can be made much simpler with a thesaurus.

Step 1
Look up one of the words – for example, 'bursting' – in the section at the back which is like a dictionary. This is what it says under 'burst':

burst
break 46 vb.
be dispersed 75 vb.
be violent 176 vb.
open 263 vb.
spurt 277 n.
be brittle 330 vb.
bang 402 vb.
activity 678 n.

Step 2

Look down the list and decide which of the 'keywords' listed comes closest to the meaning that you want, and is also the right word class.

In this case, it might be worth looking up *be violent*, *spurt*, and *bang*, all of which sound as though they might be found in a poem about fireworks.

Step 3

Begin, for example, with *be violent*, which will be found in section (not page) 176. When we turn to that section, we find the following:

Looking through the verbs (the paragraph headed **Vb.**), we find the following suggestions, which could be useful in writing the poem:

tear, hurtle, surge, storm, rage, roar, foam, explode, erupt.

Step 4

Look up the second keyword, *spurt*, and any others, until you arrive at a list of useful words and phrases for your poem.

Now use a thesaurus to find words related to some of the other suggestions on page 63. You might begin with *shivering*, *whirling*, and *showering*.

---

176. Violence – N. *violence,* vehemence, frenzy, impetuosity 174 *vigorousness*; destructiveness 165 *destruction*; boisterousness, turbulence 318 *commotion*; bluster, uproar, riot, row, roughhouse 61 *turmoil*; roughness, rough handling 735 *severity*; force, hammer blows, high hand, strong-arm tactics, thuggery, terrorism 735 *brute force*; atrocity, outrage, torture 898 *cruel act*; barbarity, brutality, savagery, blood lust 898 *inhumanity*; fierceness, ferocity 906 *pitilessness*; rage, hysterics 822 *excitable state*; fit, throes, paroxysm, spasm; shock, clash 279 *collision*.

outbreak, outburst, ebullition 318 *agitation*; flood, cataclysm, convulsion, earthquake, tremor 149 *revolution*; eruption, explosion, burst, blast 165 *destruction*; detonation; rush, onrush 712 *attack*; gush, spurt, jet, torrent.

storm, turmoil, turbulence, war of the elements; weather, dirty w., rough w.; squall, tempest, typhoon, hurricane, cyclone 352 *gale*; thunder, thunder and lightning, fulguration; rainstorm, cloudburst 350 *rain*; blizzard 380 *wintriness*.

violent creature, brute, beast, wild b.; dragon, tiger, wolf, mad dog; demon, hellhound 938 *monster*; savage 168 *destroyer*; he-man, cave m. 372 *male*; butcher 362 *murderer*; berserker, homicidal maniac; tough, rowdy, thug, mugger 904 *ruffian*; hooligan, bully 735 *tyrant*; thunderer, fire-eater 877 *boaster*; fire-brand 738 *agitator*; revolutionary, terrorist; hotspur, madcap 857 *desperado*; virago, termagant; spitfire, fury 892 *shrew*.

Adj. *violent,* vehement, forcible 162 *strong*; acute 256 *sharp*; unmitigated; excessive 32 *exorbitant*; rude, ungentle, extreme, severe, heavy-handed 735 *oppressive*; savage, brutal, bloody 898 *cruel*; hotblooded 892 *irascible*; aggressive, bellicose 718 *warlike*; struggling, kicking, thrashing about 61 *disorderly*; rough, wild, furious, raging, blustery, tempestuous, stormy, uproarious, obstreperous 400 *loud*; rowdy, turbulent, tumultuous, boisterous 738 *riotous*; intemperate, immoderate, unbridled, unrestrained; ungovernable, unruly, uncontrollable 738

disobedient; irrepressible, inextinguishable 174 *vigorous*; ebullient, inflamed, fiery 381 *heated*; explosive, eruptive, cataclysmic, volcanic, seismic 165 *destructive*; convulsive 318 *agitated*; disturbed, troublous 61 *orderless*.

furious, fuming, boiling, towering; infuriated, mad, maddened 891 *angry*; rampant, roaring, howling; impetuous, headstrong 680 *hasty*; desperate, savage, tameless, wild; blustering, threatening 899 *cursing*; vicious, fierce, ferocious 898 *cruel*; bloodthirsty, ravening, rabid, berserk 362 *murderous*; frantic, hysterical, in hysterics 503 *frenzied*.

Vb. be violent, break bounds, run wild, run riot, run amok 165 *lay waste*; tear, rush, dash, hurtle, hurl oneself 277 *move fast*; crash in 297 *burst in*; surge forward, stampede, mob 712 *charge*; riot, rough-house, kick up a shindy, raise the dust, go on the rampage 61 *rampage*; resort to violence 718 *go to war*, 738 *revolt*; see red, go berserk 891 *be angry*; storm, rage, roar, bluster 352 *blow*; ferment, foam, fume, boil over, effervesce; explode, go off, blow up, detonate, burst, flash, flare; let fly, fulminate; erupt, break out, fly o., burst o., struggle, scratch, bite, kick, lash out; savage, maul 655 *wound*; tyrannize, out-Herod Herod 735 *oppress*.

force, use f., smash 46 *break*; tear 46 *sunder*; crush 332 *pulverize*; blow up 165 *demolish*; strain, wrench, twist 246 *distort*; force open, blow open, prize o. 263 *open*; shake 318 *agitate*; do violence to 675 *mis-use*; violate, ravish, rape; torture 645 *ill-treat*.

make violent, stir 821 *excite*; goad, lash, whip 612 *incite*; inflame, add fuel to the flames 381 *heat*; foment, exacerbate 832 *aggravate*; whet 256 *sharpen*; irritate, infuriate, madden 891 *enrage*.

Adv. *violently,* forcibly, by storm, by force, with might and main; tooth and nail, hammer and tongs; at the point of a sword, at the end of a gun; bodily, neck and crop; at one fell swoop; with a vengeance, like mad; precipitately, headlong, slap bang, wham; head first; like a bull at a gate, like Gadarene swine.

Where the English Language Came From

The story of Beowulf and Grendel, which you read an extract from on page 75, is actually around 1200 years old. It was originally written in a language spoken by people known as Anglo-Saxons who had settled in England around the middle of the fifth century. Their earlier home had been on the mainland of northern Europe. That is why their language (known as Old English or Anglo-Saxon) looks and sounds a bit like German or Dutch.

Below is another extract from the *Beowulf* poem – just after the wounded Grendel has fled – as it originally looked in Old English. A word-for-word translation has been written on the opposite page. But before reading it, try the following in pairs:

Looking at the alphabet

1 This extract contains all the modern letters which existed in Old English except k, which wasn't used much. Work out which modern English letters did not exist in Old English. (There were four.)

2 Look at the words which contain letters which we no longer have in modern English. They include:
   - æ called 'ash' and pronounced like the *a* in *cat*;
   - ð and þ called 'eth' and 'thorn' which both made the *th* sounds in *thin* and *then*. You should now be able to decipher the odd-looking first word of the extract.

Looking at the vocabulary

Most of the commonest words we use today come from Old English. Find the Old English versions of the following modern English words and discuss how much (or how little) the words have changed:

that was token hand arm and there all under roof in morning my many

þæt wæs tacen sweotol,
syþðan hildedeor hond alegde,
earm ond eaxle – þær wæs eal geador
Grendles grape – under geapne hrof.
ða wæs on morgen mine gefræge
ymb þa gifhealle guðrinc monig.

Compound words

Many words in Old English are made up of two shorter words. For example, *hilde* means battle and *deor* means brave, so a *hildedeor* is a person brave in battle, or a warrior. Another word for warrior in this extract is made up of the words *guð* (war) and *rinc* (man). The third compound word is *gifhealle* (gift-hall).

There are many common words in Modern English which have been made up in exactly the same way. Think about football, bookshelf and teapot. How many other commonly used compound words can you think of?

Some words were put together so long ago that we forget that they are compounds at all. What were the origins of penknife, cupboard, and sideboard?

Here is a word-for-word literal translation of the extract on page 80 (with an understandable version in italics).

That was token clear
That was a clear sign
when brave in battle hand laid down
when the brave man laid down the hand,
arm and shoulder – there was all together
the arm and the shoulder – it was all together:
Grendel's claw – under wide roof.
Grendel's claw – under the high roof.
Then was in morning my information
Then in the morning, as I have heard, there was
around the gift-hall battlemen many.
many a warrior around the gift-hall.

Runes

Runes (from an Old English word meaning 'secret') were an alphabet of special letters designed for inscriptions which had some important or even magical meaning. This is what they looked like, together with their modern equivalents:

Some runes stood for two modern letters: NG TH EA Æ IO Œ

When you have deciphered this sentence it will still be in Old English and will have to be translated:

Giving Information
Local News

In January 1995 a huge earthquake hit the Japanese city of Kobe, killing more than 5,000 people and leaving more than 100,000 homeless.

You would expect such a major disaster to be reported in a national newspaper, but what about a local paper? Should it report an international news story, or should it stick to local issues?

Here's how two newspapers reported the story. One of them is a national paper, the other a local one:

Kobe steeled for the aftershock

From Peter McGill in Kobe

Frantic preparations were being made yesterday against the threat of heavy rain, which will further loosen the foundations of fractured buildings. Shortly after 9pm an aftershock rattled the city – a reminder of the ever-present danger of further quakes.

With a magnitude of 7.1 on the Richter scale, the Southern Hyogo Earthquake on Tuesday was more than twice as powerful as that in Los Angeles, exactly one year before. In intensity it gave the uppermost reading of 7 on a Japanese scale of measurement, the highest ever recorded.

Independent on Sunday,
22 January 1995

Ex-York vicar survives quake

A former York vicar is helping survivors of the devastating earthquake in Japan.

The Reverend Peter Jackson has been in Kobe for three years and was there when the earthquake struck on Monday night.

His son Mark, 26, of Milson Grove, York, said he could not believe it when he watched the news and saw the death toll mounting.

'It is still not 100 per cent safe out there but my father runs the Mission for Seamen which is being used as a rallying point,' he added.

Yorkshire Evening Press,
20 January 1995

The two extracts show one of the differences between national and local newspapers. In this case the local paper reports an international event, but manages to find a local 'angle'.

Local versus national

1 Do you agree with this approach to reporting the news, or do you think the local paper makes the disaster seem trivial or small-scale?

2 What do you think each type of newspaper is actually for? In your view, how should a local paper be different from a national one?

3 Sort out your opinion by looking at these different statements from newspaper readers. Then discuss which you most agree and disagree with:

The national newspaper gives the facts, but it's quite boring. The local paper at least gives a flavour of the human side of the disaster.

The local paper is right to show how a national story can have an impact on local people.

Local papers are about local issues: it should not have mentioned the international story at all.

The national paper gives the facts; the local paper is laughable: it's just trying to find a local story in a major disaster.

Newspaper survey

1 Once you have discussed which of the statements you most agree with, use the following survey to decide upon your 'ideal' local newspaper. What should it contain and how local should it be?

Aside from the items listed in the survey, what else should it contain?

- horoscopes
- education news
- reviews (theatre/cinema/music/software)
- cartoons
- business news
- campaigns (e.g. to improve safety on the streets)
- anything else?

2 Compare your answers with other people's in your class. What similarities and differences are there in what people want from a local newspaper? How local do most people want it to be?

If you were to buy a local newspaper every day, what would you want it to contain?

For each answer, use the 1 to 5 scale to show how local a local paper should be.

1 news stories   yes/no

HOW LOCAL?	1 all local	2	3 mostly local/ some national	4	5 local + plenty of national/international

2 sports   yes/no

HOW LOCAL?	1 all local	2	3 mostly local/ some national	4	5 local + plenty of national/international

3 interviews with people in the news   yes/no

HOW LOCAL?	1 all local	2	3 mostly local/ some national	4	5 local + plenty of national/international

4 opinion columns   yes/no

HOW LOCAL?	1 all local	2	3 mostly local/ some national	4	5 local + plenty of national/international

5 entertainment guides (TV listings/music/theatre/cinema etc)   yes/no

HOW LOCAL?	1 all local	2	3 mostly local/ some national	4	5 local + plenty of national/international

Making News 1

Now here's your chance to put some of your ideas into practice. Working in a group of four or five, you are the editorial team of a local newspaper. Use the information below to put together your front page. To do this you will need to be able to:

- work to a deadline
- make fast decisions about which stories to include and which to leave out
- devise the most eye-catching layout for the paper
- write accurate stories quickly

The unit is in two parts:

1 a briefing about what you will be required to do
2 resources for your next lesson

News briefing

In your next English lesson you will need to work quickly to put together the front page of a local newspaper. News stories will be coming in all the time, from a variety of sources. To cope with them, you will need to be able to work as a team and know exactly what role each of you is playing.

Decide today:

1 whether you want the front page to be completely local, chiefly local/partly national, or mostly national
2 what roles you will each take: editor, designer, sub-editor, journalist
3 what sort of layout you will use for your front page

BASICS

Task: to put together the front page of a local newspaper, *The Local Leader*

Time: 1 lesson
Group: 4 or 5 people

Resources you will need:
* A3 paper (or two sheets of A4 stuck together)
* writing tools (e.g. pencils, pens, word processors)
* scissors and glue sticks for pasting stories onto the front page
* TV and video (optional)

Roles

Editor
You will discuss ideas for the paper with the team, but the final decision about what makes the front page is yours. You are responsible for getting the paper produced on time. Under pressure of time you are likely also to help write articles.

Designer
The final look of the front page is yours: you decide which page format to use, which photographs and where, how much advertising space and where.

Sub-editor
You do the cutting and pasting – placing articles onto the finished page, cutting articles where necessary, and adding headlines and sub-headings.

Journalist(s)
You take the information and write the stories, working quickly to try and give an accurate story which will interest the reader. Use the facts you are given, but for this exercise you may also add some details of your own.

Layout

Two different possible layouts are suggested. You could use these as models for your group's front page.

Note that no drawing of pictures is necessary – in the space for photographs you simply write a description of what will go there. This will allow you to concentrate on the text and layout, rather than spend time drawing pictures or cutting out photos.

Discuss what you like and dislike about each page layout. Which will your team use?

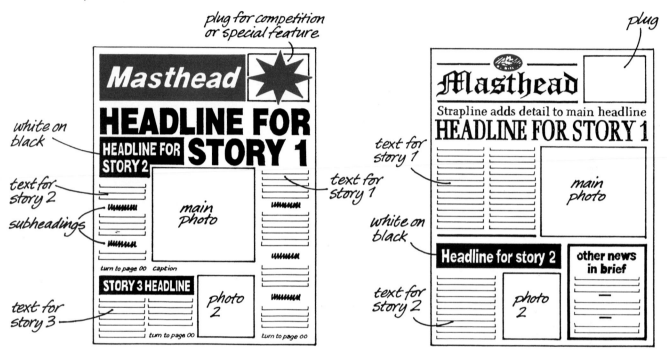

Making preparations

At the start of your next lesson, you will receive several news agency reports. These are stories wired to you from local, national, and international news-gathering offices. You need to decide which you will use and where they will go on the front page. Some stories may be presented to you on paper; others are printed in this book. If you are using the video, some stories will also be flashed up on the screen.

As a team, you need to sort the stories, write up the ones you want to use, and get them onto the front page. The deadline will be fixed by your teacher. You should aim to have the paper 'put to bed' by then.

Decide now:

1 What will you do if a late story breaks?

2 Will local stories always be more important than national ones?

If you have any time left over now, discuss:
- the kind of paper you want to produce
- who it is aimed at
- what kind of stories you will run
- whether there are any national and international stories which would make your front page …

You could also use any remaining time to ask questions about what will happen in the next lesson – you're not going to have time for anything but producing your paper.

Making News 2

You have this lesson to create a newspaper front page for *The Local Leader*. Spend your time gathering the news, deciding which stories you will use, writing them up, and pasting them onto your front page.

News Agency Reports

.00... Severe flooding reported in your area with several homes threatened by the River Flotsam bursting its bank. Police are evacuating 200 homes in the immediate area. Water spokesperson Milda Bethell says 'Weather forecasts are not looking hopeful. There could be more flooding tonight' ...

.01... National Lottery plunged into chaos as the computerized network is hit by a major system failure. Millions of people turned away when buying their tickets. This weekend's jackpot could be the lowest ever. Lottery spokesperson Stephen Joseph said 'We apologize for the problem and hope to have the error rectified within 24 hours' ...

.02... Australian outback on fire as flames are fanned by 60 mph winds. Now threatening Adelaide. Residents are refusing to leave their homes after last year's false alarm ...

.03... Sneezy the kitten lives up to her name by sneezing every time she is petted by humans. Sneezy is so cute that everyone wants to cuddle her, but that just sets off her sneezing attacks. Owner Nigel Strensall from your area says they are seeking medical advice ...

.04... Opposition motion in the House of Commons means that tonight's all-night sitting of Parliament could turn into a vote of no confidence. If that happened the Government might not hold its majority and a general election could be called. Opposition sources say 'We are confident that the Government will be gone within a matter of weeks' ...

.05... Dally Pond, star of the new hit TV soap <u>Night Life</u>, visited your area today to open a new supermarket. She visited patients at a local hospital and answered questions about her forthcoming autobiography, <u>Beneath the Suds</u> ...

.06... Thieves in your area today stole a Ford Escort parked outside 72 Cleveland Way. The owner, Rachel Hammond, was visiting her aunt and had left the car unlocked whilst she unpacked groceries ...

News review

After the lesson, review:

1 how far you got
2 what problems you faced
3 how your news values compare with other groups' (Did you all lead with the same main story?)
4 how you worked as a team
5 how you might have been more successful

Taking it further

Write an account of the way your team put their front page together, using the points listed above in 'News Review'. Give examples of the decisions you made and the difficulties you faced. Use this paragraph plan to help:

Introduction
- who was in your group
- who took which role and how you decided this
- what you discussed at your first meeting

Planning the paper
- discussions about what a local newspaper should contain
- decisions about layout
- other points you decided in advance

Making news
- how you felt before you started working to deadline
- what your job involved
- how everyone reacted to problems
- how you decided which stories to use
- other decisions the team made
- how you worked to the deadline

Conclusion
- what went right
- what went wrong
- what your team could have done better
- what you liked and disliked about the project

Magazines
What Makes a Magazine?

Walk into any newsagent's shop or supermarket and, above the newspapers, you will probably see hundreds of magazines on display.

Charting the differences

What makes a magazine different from a newspaper?

1 Working in a pair, look at this list of suggestions and add your own ideas in the spaces.
2 What other differences can you think of? Add them to the chart.

Newspapers are usually ...	Magazines are usually ...
produced daily or weekly	
quickly thrown away	
	glossy
full of news	
	aimed at specific audiences (e.g. golfers, young women, wrestling fans)
written chiefly to <u>inform</u>	

Women's Magazines

Look at this list of magazine titles aimed at women readers. How many have you heard of or seen?

Women's magazines are aimed at different target audiences – for instance, at young working women, or at older women with families.

Some aim to be highly fashionable; others aim to be traditional.

Annabel	19
Bella	Options
Best	People's Friend
Chat	Prima
Company	She
Cosmopolitan	Take a Break
Elle	Tatler
Essentials	The Lady
Family Circle	True Romances
Good Housekeeping	True Stories
Harpers & Queen	Vogue
Hello	Woman
Living	Woman and Home
Looks	Woman's Journal
Marie Claire	Woman's Own
Me	Woman's Realm
More!	Woman's Story
My Weekly	Woman's Weekly
New Woman	

Looking at names

1 Working in groups of four, read the list again. What can you tell about the magazines from their titles? Which would you predict are aimed at a fashion audience and which at a more traditional one? Try to regroup the titles into columns like the ones on the right.

2 Now take the titles in your 'Younger audience' box and number them to show which *sounds* the most fashionable and which *sounds* the least. Give the most fashionable title 1, the next 2, and so on. Discuss in your group what it is in the magazine titles which makes them feel fashionable.

3 Do the same for the 'Traditional audience' box, ordering the titles from most to least traditional. Again, discuss what clues in the titles make you class them as more or less traditional than others.

Younger audience	Traditional audience	Not sure

Selling the image: TV commercials

Watch the three TV commercials for women's magazines – *Eva*, *Chat*, and *Woman's Weekly*. For each commercial, note down your thoughts on the following questions:

Audience

1 Which women do you think the magazines are aimed at – women with families? Single women? What age? What kinds of interests?

Style

2 What do you notice about the way the commercials have been produced?
   - Do they use facts or stories to advertise the magazines?
   - What kind of music do they use?
   - What are the characters like in them? What are they doing? Are they happy, under pressure, relaxed?
   - Does the commercial feel fast-moving, exciting, relaxing, or neutral?

3 What message do you think each commercial is giving about each magazine? What key point is it stressing?

Your impression

4 What do you like or dislike about each commercial? How would you improve it? Which magazine would you prefer to buy, based on the commercials?

91

A New Magazine

You are part of a team that is about to launch a new fashion magazine for a teenage market. This is the brief that you have been given by your publisher:

PRICELESS
PUBLISHING

MEMO

From   E. Morrow, Publisher
To   Marketing Team

This magazine is completely new and the readers are going to love it! What's radically different is that we're aiming to get teenagers talking about fashion. But instead of just aiming at females or just aiming at males, we're going to produce a magazine which they'll all want to read!

It will contain celebrities in state-of-the-art clothing. It will have fashion features. There will be loads of hot colour photos and lively, entertaining text.

It will show its audience that everyone – males and females – should take an interest in their appearance, and give solid, affordable advice on how to feel better about your looks.

Sounds good?

Of course it does – but we need a name to launch …

Over to you!

Name game

Your team has begun to think of titles for the new magazine. Using the ideas below as a starting-point, work in threes or fours to come up with a name that will fit the magazine's image.

The Look!	Discovery	Psssss!
Secrets	Focal Point	About You
Being	Garb!	Lifestyle

For each title, discuss:

1 what you like or dislike about it
2 how well it fits the new magazine's image
3 whether it suggests other types of magazines instead
4 any other titles you can think of

At the end of the discussion, you should have a magazine title which you feel confident will grab the attention of the target audience. Present it to the rest of your class.

92

Magazines: Past and Present

The secret of success

As you can see from the table, the most successful magazines today sell more than a million copies per issue.

1 Why do you think people enjoy reading magazines so much? Decide which of the statements below you most agree with.

2 If you look back at magazines from the start of this century, they contained few pictures and no colour. Yet people still read them. Can you think of other reasons besides those listed here?

FACT FILE

Best-selling women's magazines (1990)

Bella	1,191,189
Woman's Weekly	1,067,382
Take a Break	924,634
Woman's Own	830,086
Woman	805,511
Me	733,412
Best	679,349
Prima	673,871

Magazines are easy to read – you can roll them up, keep them in a pocket or bag, and it doesn't matter too much if they get creased.

Magazines are designed to be flicked through – the layout, use of colour and large number of pictures make you want to read them.

Magazines encourage a lazy approach to reading – they don't need any effort.

Magazines let you read in short bursts – you can just dip into them. This makes them much easier to read than a novel.

Past or present?

Look at the eight magazine extracts over the page. All are taken from two magazines aimed at teenage girls – one was written in 1994, the other in 1937. Can you tell the old from the new based purely on the language?

In pairs, read each extract and decide whether it is from the 1990s or the 1930s. Then write down the clues that helped you decide – precisely which words and why. Answers are in the Teacher's Book.

	1990s	1930s	Clues
1			
2			
3			
4			
5			
6			
7			
8			

1

Your mum and dad will want to know all about your new school and how you're getting on. Keep them informed and up-to-date – they're just concerned about how you're coping with this new experience.

2

On your first couple of days you'll be bombarded with information, directions and loads of textbooks. It can all seem a bit overwhelming but the worst thing you can do is panic. It will all fall into place.

3

Here's a little catch with figures that you can try out on the girl sitting next to you in school, before lessons begin.
Your voice must be casual, and you mustn't linger over this catch, for once you give her time to think it over, she'll probably see through it.
'How d'you write eleven thousand, eleven hundred and eleven?' you ask seriously.
Unless she's frightfully bright (or has heard the catch before!) you'll see her start to write things that'll probably go like this: 11,1111, or 11,111—'

4

Don't pay too much attention to rumours you hear about school before you actually start. Older pupils love to terrify new ones with scary stories about terrible teachers, work so difficult it's impossible and homework that takes hours. It can't be that bad, otherwise no one would last, would they?

5

Four inches, six inches, or even eight inches from the ground when kneeling – whatever the official school length your tunic is supposed to be, there will come a time when it's just too hopelessly short, and you'll be glad to turn it into something else.

6

At high school you're expected to take more responsibility for yourself. If you don't understand something, don't be afraid to ask. If you don't you'll end up falling behind and getting into a panic.

7

It's a good idea to jot down important info about your timetable, textbooks etc. Writing things down helps you remember.
Getting lots of homework can seem a nightmare. The key is to organize yourself and not put it off until the last minute – that's a recipe for disaster!

8

Oh, and here's a little riddle I've found for you – one that you really should try out on the brainiest girl in the class, for it sounds such a serious question. (You who know all about light travelling at 186,000 miles a second and sound at 11,000 feet a second, will appreciate it especially.)
You say, with a wide-eyed expression, to the brainy one:
'Which travels faster, heat or cold?'
Unless you've picked the wrong girl to ask, and she starts chasing you, she'll be stumped, or want to start looking it up in her science books.
'Why, heat does, you silly, 'cause you can catch cold!' you laugh, and then prepare to dash.
Good, though, isn't it?

From past to present

How would you go about updating a 1930s article to the 1990s? Is it possible? Take this short extract from *The Schoolgirl* about sunbathing, and have a go at writing a similar article for a modern teenage audience. You will want to change:

- some of the language (including the heading)
- some of the ideas
- the writer's style

Change the original as much as you like: just try to write a modern article about sunbathing which gives advice on sun protection, peeling, avoiding the sun, and so on.

You might start off: 'If you like nothing better than to bask in the sun on a sizzling summer's day, then …'

Then compare your rewritten version with those of others in your group.

A SUN-BATH IS SO GOOD FOR YOU

A GENTLE START

If you are an out-of-doors girl and have been playing around in the air and sun a good deal this finer weather, you'll be pretty tough.

But if you're more the hothouse plant type of girl, then your skin will be sensitive.

The out-of-doors girl may bask in the sun for as long as an hour without going red and blistery.

But the girl with pale, sensitive skin should sun-bathe only for ten minutes for the first time. I know this sounds very hard, but it honestly is quite serious – for an overdose of sun can do real harm.

Too much sun on the back of the neck can make you very dizzy and give quite an ill-feeling – while too much on the arms can produce the most painful blistering – followed by ugly 'peeling'.

BROWN-MAKING

Ordinary olive oil – or salad oil for that matter – rubbed into the arms and legs is marvellous for attracting the sun and encouraging tan.

I shouldn't use this on the face, though, if I were you. That will brown much more readily than the rest of you, never having been covered.

But I do suggest that you give your face an extra little treat after the sun-bath. It will very likely have a 'tight', skin-stretched feeling, which is actually caused by the sun drying up a lot of the natural oils.

So you should replace these, simply by smearing cold cream over your face and allowing it to stay on for a few minutes, if possible. You'll be surprised at how much the skin will have absorbed – which shows how much it needed this – and any extra can be wiped off with an old piece of rag.

Taking it further

Which magazines do you enjoy? Or which do you loathe? Write a personal account of one such magazine, describing what it's about, how it is presented, features you especially like/dislike, and who you think it is aimed at. When did you begin reading it (at what age?), and what do you like about it that can't be found in newspapers or books?

Persuading People
Handwriting Styles

Your own handwriting

With a partner, discuss how you feel about your own handwriting. Which of these words and phrases best describes it?

scruffy	eye-catching
small	full of character
neat	clear
attractive	difficult to read
unusual	careful
childish	

What is special or distinctive about your handwriting style? Which letters do you form in a particular way? How is your handwriting different from your friends' styles? Whose handwriting do you admire? What do you like about their style of writing?

A matter of style

Graphologists are people who study handwriting. They say that the way someone writes can tell us what that person is like. Many other people say that it's all a lot of nonsense. What do you think?

Here are some sentences from five Year 8 students, written about teachers who have influenced them. They are followed by a printed statement each one made about their personality. Working in a pair, can you match the handwriting to the personality statements using these guidelines from handwriting experts?

HANDWRITING CLUES

1 **Slant**
   - A slant to the left can show someone who is basically shy.
   - A slant to the right can show someone who is out-going and enjoys company.
   - Upright writing can show someone who is coolly independent and self-confident.
   - Mixed slants can suggest someone who is moody and changeable. Pop stars and artists often write like this!

2 **Style**
   - Connected (joined-up) script can show someone who is logical and thoughtful.
   - Disconnected writing can show someone who likes to work alone and be independent.
   - A combination of the styles can show someone who has creative and intellectual ability – writers, artists, and scientists often have this style.

3 **Size**
   - Large handwriting can show self-confidence. Very large, fancy writing may show writers who like to attract attention to themselves.
   - Small handwriting may suggest excellent organizing ability.

The handwriting

A

My 4th year teacher Mr Baxter. He I was really shy at first but Mr Baxter made the whole class confident about coming into secondary school.

B

Miss Christopher has had the most positive effect on me by making me more confident and teaches the first English class I have ever liked because we do more interesting things.

C

Mrs Graham was my primary teacher from primary four till primary seven and she always encouraged me to do my best and made sure I always happy.

D

The teacher who has had the most positive influence on me was my last teacher at Primary School, Mr. Bowman (New Earswick Primary School) He prepared me well for secondary school and I felt he brought out my character and gave me much confidence. His jolly, humourous personality made me feel at ease at school and his humour had a large effect on my personality. I could write several sides of A5 paper on this person who had an enormous influence on me but I think I should stop now!

E

Mr. Collianton. Mr. Mrs. Cadell. Because she helped me too learn English in the infants.

Personality descriptions

1

I am quite outgoing but at the same time a bit shy when I'm in the company of strangers. I like to have a laugh with people I know well. I'm enthusiastic about most things (usually) but I can become very moody.

2

I am thoughtful. I am boring. I like to work on my own.

3

1. I am an organized person.
2. I am outgoing.
3. I like working in teams rather than on my own.

4

I am happy quite a lot of the time and easily pleased (sometimes). I am absolutely mad about animals, especially dogs. I love music and can play lots of instruments. Tidiness can annoy me.

5

My personality is I can be shy sometimes. I am mostly organized.

Of course, this isn't a very scientific experiment. A graphologist would say that you need training before you can properly analyse someone's handwriting. But you might find it interesting to look at the way you form certain letters. Read what graphologist Patricia Marne says about them:

Graphology

Small a

a a a a a a a a a a a a
1 2 3 4 5 6 7 8 9 10 11 12

1 Closed: Discreet, diplomatic
2 Open at top: Talkative
3 Closed and knotted: Secretive
4 Narrow: Narrow-minded
5 Loop to right: Tactful
6 Loop to left: Self-deceitful
7 Broad oval: Imaginative
8 Open at bottom: Dishonest
9 Filled in: Jealous
10 Square: Mechanically-minded
11 Open at left: Egoistic, greedy
12 Amendments: Nervous

Small b

b b b b b b b b b b b b
1 2 3 4 5 6 7 8 9 10 11 12

1 Like figure 6: Familiar with figures
2 Long starting stroke: Fussy
3 Without loop: Intelligent
4 Looped initial stroke: Proud
5 Looped on end stroke: Imaginative
6 Printed: Literary
7 Rounded starting stroke: Humorous
8 With hook: Obstinate
9 Enrolled: Greedy, egoistical
10 Pointed tops: Resentful
11 Amendments: Neurotic
12 Initial tick: Persistent

Small k

k k k k k k k k like
1 2 3 4 5 6 7 8 9

1 Large loop to right: Rebellious
2 High narrow loop: Religious
3 Knotted: Proud, thorough
4 Stroke going down: Defensive
5 Printed: Literary
6 Underlining stroke: Self-loving
7 Stroke extended at top: Enterprising
8 High and wide loop: Emotional
9 Written as a capital
within a word: Mildly eccentric

Small l

l l l l l l l
1 2 3 4 5 6 7

1 High and wide: Emotional, sensitive
2 Very high: Visionary
3 No loop: Good judgement
4 Inflated upper loop: Generous
5 Pointed at top: High aspirations
6 Zero form: Interested in money
7 Sharp at bottom: Obstinate

Patricia Marne

Do you agree?

1 Look at the examples and discuss which letters are closest to yours. Look at your exercise book for examples of the way you write certain letters. Do you agree with the descriptions given?

2 Look at a friend's lettering. Based on these examples, what can you tell about their personality from their handwriting?

Making Judgements

How important do you think handwriting style is? Would it influence you if you were appointing someone to a job? Test your own attitude now.

Imagine you are the boss of Scarfe Sandpits Ltd, a company that sells outdoor play equipment to toy shops. You have advertised the post of Factory Manager in the newspaper and the applications have begun to arrive.

First impressions

Look at the endings from these typewritten or word-processed letters below. Focus on what the writer says.

Which two of the five applicants would you call to interview? Why? What is it in the extracts from their letters that you like/dislike?

Then see if your decision would be the same based on their handwritten letters, over the page.

I feel confident that my management experience has fully prepared me for this challenging and dynamic position. I look forward to hearing from you.

Yours sincerely,

Penny Todd

I also have a young nephew who enjoys playing in sandpits, which is another reason why I would really like to work for you company.

Yours sincerely,

Martin Rendell

C

I really hope that you will call me to interview because I would be delighted to talk more about the job and what it entails.

Yours,

Sam Strickland

I know that my qualification don't look perfect on paper, but I know that I could do it and I will work hard to do it well. I hope you will give me the chance of proving this to you at interview.

Best wishes,

Yours sincerely,

K. Samms

For all of these reasons I feel that I am well qualified for the post on offer. The job itself, the reputation of the company, and the salary on offer all make it feel like the ideal appointment for me. I hope very much that I might have the opportunity of discussing my application with you more in person.

Yours sincerely,

F. Brigshaw.

Second thoughts

Look at the same application letters written in different handwriting styles and see whether you would be influenced by the appearance of the letters. Would you still call the same two applicants to interview?

B

I also have a young nephew who enjoys playing in sandpits, which is another reason why I would really like to work for you company.

Yours sincerely,

Martin Rendell.

A

I feel confident that my management experience has fully prepared me for this challenging and dynamic position. I look forward to hearing from you.

Yours sincerely,

Penny Todd

D

I know that my qualification don't look perfect on paper, but I know that I could do it and I will work hard to do it well. I hope you will give me the chance of proving this to you at interview.

Best wishes,

Yours sincerely,

K. Samms.

C

I really hope that you will call me to interview because I would be delighted to talk more about the job & what it entails –

Yours,

Sam Strickland –

E

For all of these reasons I feel that I am well qualified for the post on offer. The job itself, the reputation of the company, and the salary on offer all make it feel like the ideal appointment for me. I hope very much that I might have the opportunity to discussing my application with you more in person.

Yours sincerely,

F. Brigshaw.

Content versus style

1 Place the letters in rank order using a table like this one. Use it to show which letter is best in terms of
- content (what it says/how well the writer expresses him or herself)
- handwritten style (which style you find most/least attractive)

	Content of letter	Handwriting style
1 = best		
2		
3		
4		
5 = worst		

Do you get the same results each time? Is the best letter, in your opinion, the one with the best content, or does presentation play a part?

2 Compare your results with other people's in the group. What conclusions can you draw?

- Which one of the candidates would you invite to interview? Why?
- How important is the writer's handwriting in your decision?
- Which is more important to you – content or handwritten style?

Taking it further

Write a personal account about your own attitude to writing. Use these questions to structure your ideas:

- What memories do you have of being taught to write?
- Are there some times when you love writing and others when you hate it?
- Are there some subjects in which you enjoy writing more than in others?
- What are your ideal writing conditions – where? what kind of desk? what kind of pen? word-processor?
- What, precisely, do you like and dislike about your own handwriting style?

Media Texts

Image-making

How do food and drink companies persuade us to buy their product instead of a rival brand? The answer is by creating an image for their product and then advertising it.

Test your reactions

In pairs, put that to the test by answering the following questions.

1 If buying a cola drink in a supermarket, which brand would you be most likely to buy?

2 If that brand were not available, which would you buy next?

3 Which brands would you definitely *not* buy?

4 If there was a special offer on the supermarket's own brand of cola, would you buy that rather than your normal cola? Why/why not?

5 Now look at these products. For each one, guess which two or three brands are the biggest sellers:

- breakfast cereals
- sweets
- fizzy drinks
- pet foods
- crisps

Discuss your answers with your partner. How much do you both rely on the reputation of well-known brand-names?

Best-selling brands

With a partner, read this article from *The Guardian* newspaper, then discuss any surprises in the list of favourites. Are there products here which you think are terrible or which you have never heard of? Are there popular brands which are not mentioned?

Real thing for Coke as sales top league

Coca-Cola dominates a league table of Britain's top-selling brands, with more than £350 million worth of sales last year, a survey has found.

Persil and Ariel soap powders were second and third in the table, but well below Coke with sales worth around £210 million each.

They were followed by, in order of sales, Nescafe coffee, Whiskas cat food – both more than £170 million – Walkers Crisps, Bell's Special Old Scotch, PG Tips tea, Flora margarine and Tetley tea.

New entrants to the annual survey's league table of the top 50 brands in grocery stores were Muller Yoghurt, Golden Wonder Pots, Lenor Fabric Conditioner,

Bird's Eye Frozen Peas and St Ivel Shape Yogurt.

Out of the top 50 were Co-op 99 Tea, John West Salmon, McVitie's Chocolate Homewheat, Bisto, and Country Life Butter.

The report was compiled by market researchers Nielsen and published in Marketing Magazine.

Our favourite food and drink

■ Kellogg's Corn Flakes was the top seller among breakfast cereals, the survey found. It was followed by, in order of popularity, Weetabix, Frosties, Crunchy Nut Corn Flakes, Rice Krispies, Kellogg's Bran Flakes, Shredded Wheat, Special K, All Bran, and Kellogg's Variety Packs.

■ Kit Kat heads the sweets league,

followed by Mars Bar, Cadbury's Dairy Milk, Twix, Roses, Quality Street, Snickers, Aero Milk Chocolate, Maltesers, and Bounty.

■ After Coke and Pepsi, the next favourite fizzy drinks were Lucozade, Tango, Schweppes Mixers, Lilt, 7-up, Irn Bru, Sunkist, and Sprite.

■ The top pet food brands are Whiskas, Pedigree Chum, Arthur's, Felix, Prime, Pal, Kit-e-Kat, Cesar, Choosy, and Chappie.

■ Walkers Crisps last year sold more than twice as much as its nearest rival, Golden Wonder. Hula Hoops, Quavers, KP Peanuts, Skips, Wotsits, McCoys, Monster Munch and Discos were the next most popular brands.

The Guardian

Selling the image

What different images do the different products have? What makes them appeal to the buyer?

1 Choose one category – breakfast cereals, sweets, fizzy drinks, pet foods, or crisps. Make a list of each of the product names mentioned in the newspaper article.

2 Against each name in your list, jot down notes about what is unusual, special, or memorable about the product. For the moment try to ignore its packaging and focus on just the product and its name. Use these prompts to help you.

- What precisely is the product? (e.g. is it all chocolate or does it have biscuit or caramel ingredients?)
- How does it differ from one of its rivals? (e.g. compare Mars® and KitKat)
- What one feature do you most remember about the product?
- What associations does its name have? (e.g. Cadbury's Dairy Milk hints at natural ingredients fresh from the countryside.) What images do the words of the product name conjure up in your mind?
- What do the advertisers suggest we will gain by buying this product (e.g. energy, happiness, success, value-for-money)?

KitKat	
Mars Bar	
Cadbury's Dairy Milk	Pure milk chocolate, fresh ingredients, country image
Bounty	

3 Now look at the packaging of the products. What image is created by the way the words are designed? Look at the shapes given to words, straight and curved lettering styles, and use of colour. Make notes on the images the different designs create.

Naming the product

Remembering the importance of a product's name, with a partner read over these background notes on why certain brand-names were chosen for soft drinks:

Fanta: from the German word *fantasie* (fantasy)

Kia-Ora: Maori word meaning 'good health' – exotic name perhaps suggests an exotic product

Pepsi: originally designed to relieve dyspepsia (stomach upset) but also has links with the phrase 'pepping you up'

Ribena: Latin name for blackcurrant is *ribes nigrum*

Do you know the background to any other product names?

Taking it further

Use your notes to decide what the USP (Unique Selling Point) is for each of the products you have chosen – the one special feature that makes it different from other brands on the market. It could be the product itself, or it could be the image it conjures up. Use an OHP or a large sheet of paper to present your conclusions to the rest of the group.

103

The Coca-Cola Story

If you had to say which was the most famous soft drink in the world, you would probably say 'Coca-Cola'. How much do you know about this well-known drink and the way it is advertised?

Look at this extract from the pamphlet, *The Chronicle of Coca-Cola*:

Around the turn of the century, little-known actress Hilda Clark achieved lasting fame as the attractive consumer of Coca-Cola in an array of advertising materials distributed by the Company.

BIRTH OF A REFRESHING IDEA

The product that has given the world its best-known taste was born in Atlanta, Georgia, on May 8, 1886. Dr John Styth Pemberton, a local pharmacist, produced the syrup for Coca-Cola, according to legend, in a three-legged brass pot in his backyard. He carried a jug of the new product down the street to Jacobs' Pharmacy, where it was sampled, pronounced 'excellent' and placed on sale for five cents a glass as a soda fountain drink. Whether by design or accident, carbonated water was teamed with the new syrup to produce a drink that was at once 'Delicious and Refreshing', a theme that continues to echo today wherever Coca-Cola is enjoyed.

Thinking that 'the two Cs would look well in advertising', Dr Pemberton's partner and bookkeeper, Frank M. Robinson, suggested the name and penned the now famous trademark 'Coca-Cola' in his unique script. The first newspaper ad for Coca-Cola soon appeared in *The Atlanta Journal*, inviting thirsty citizens to try 'the new and popular soda fountain drink'. Hand-painted oilcloth signs reading 'Coca-Cola' appeared on store awnings, with the suggestion 'Drink' added to inform passers-by that the new beverage was for soda fountain refreshment. During the first year, sales averaged a modest nine drinks per day.

Dr Pemberton never realized the potential of the beverage he created. He gradually sold portions of his business to various partners and, just prior to his death in 1888, sold his remaining interest in Coca-Cola to Asa G. Candler. An Atlantan with great business acumen, Mr Candler proceeded to buy additional rights and acquire complete control.

Your response

1 How much of this information about Coca-Cola did you already know?

2 Is there anything in it which surprises you?

3 Are there any clues that tell you this text was produced by The Coca-Cola Company itself?

The power of logos

Notice how Dr Pemberton liked the idea of the name 'Coca-Cola' partly because of the way it would *look*.

Advertisers often use the power of logos – letters in certain shapes – because they help us to recognize the product even if we don't actually read the words.

1 Test that for yourself: in a pair, look at these snippets of famous product logos and see if you can tell what they are. Write down what you think each product is.

2 Put together your own collage of product names, giving even smaller clues, and challenge other people in your class to say what the product names are.

Advertising: Past and Present

The Coca-Cola Company was quick to use other ways of marketing their drink – inventing a special shape for the bottle in 1916, and placing the 'Drink Coca-Cola' slogan on mirrors, calendars, glasses, trays, and even playing cards.

Coca-Cola has also used a series of different slogans or catch-phrases, often in sung jingles on TV, film, and radio commercials:

1929	The pause that refreshes
1936	It's the refreshing thing to do
1950s	Sign of good taste
1963	Things go better with Coke
1971	I'd like to buy the world a Coke
1976	Coke adds life
1979	Have a Coke and a smile
1982	Coke is it
late 1980s	Can't beat the feeling
1990s	Can't beat the real thing

From past to present

Look at the Coca-Cola advertisements below and on pages 107–8 and see if you can place them in order of oldest to most recent. Decide where each advertisement should go on the timeline. You don't have to choose an exact year (unless you want to have a go): just try to spot the decade it was created.

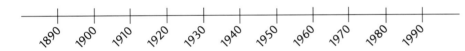

Similarities and differences

Now look at the advertisements in more detail using the prompts below:

1 Describe what features they have in common (for example, Coke logo, image of bottle, smiling face). Which two are the most similar?

2 Say what features makes each one different. Which are the most dissimilar?

3 Who do you think each advert is aimed at – teenagers, young people generally, older people, everyone? How can you tell?

4 What are the chief clues about the age of the advertisement (e.g. fashion of clothes, background details, picture style)?

5 Which of the advertisements do you like most and least? Discuss your reasons.

A

B

ΣΤΑΜΑΤΗΣΕΤΕ ΚΑΙ ΔΡΟΣΙΣΘΗΤΕ

Coca-Cola

C

BE REALLY REFRESHED...DRIVE-IN FOR COKE!

D

DRINK DELICIOUS Coca-Cola

THE COCA-COLA GIRL

E

DRINK Coca-Cola

Coca-Cola and Coke are registered trademarks which identify the same product of The Coca-Cola Company.

F

Friendly refreshment

G

Coca-Cola and Coke are registered trademarks which identify the same product of The Coca-Cola Company.

Brands on TV

Watch the soft drink commercials which appear on the video, and discuss which one you think works best.

Watch each commercial at least three times and, as you watch, make notes on the following points:

- what the storyline of the commercial is
- who each commercial seems to be aimed at (age, gender, lifestyle) – how can you tell?
- the different images the commercial uses (people, places, cartoons) – what do they all suggest about the product?
- the type of music used – what does it add? What image does it have?
- how fast-moving the commercial is – is it full of fast edits and changing images, or does it have a slower, more soothing pace? What does this suggest about the product?
- which you like best, and why

It might be useful to watch once with just the vision and another time with just the sound. This will allow you to focus more on how the commercial has been made.

Discuss your notes with others in the group. See if you agree about everyone's favourite commercial.

Taking it further

1 If you were designing a new soft drink for a young audience, what would you call it? In a group, each think of a name and slogan. Brainstorm plenty of ideas before choosing the best. Remember that an advertising agency would spend months doing this, then testing the name on members of the public. See what you can come up with in a shorter time, and then present your ideas to the rest of the class, explaining how you reached your final choice.

2 Write a report which compares the image of different brand-names within the same type of product. For example, you could compare different types of cola (supermarket versus famous-name brands) or crisps. Look at the way each product is presented and compare how successful they are. You might comment on:

■ names of the products, and their associations. What do they make you think of? Which names do you like most and least? Why?

■ the packaging of the product – modern, old-fashioned, colourful? Unusual shape of packaging? Lettering style? Who is it aimed at? Does it remind you of any other product?

■ the image the product has – popular, laughed at, neutral? Do a quick survey of people of different ages to see whether reactions to the product differ.

Summarize your findings and discuss the image of the product you like best (even if you dislike the product itself), and explain why.

Travel-writing
Brochure or Travelogue?

Look at these two definitions:

> **Travel brochure** a booklet or magazine which gives information about places people might travel to, and which tries to persuade people to go there. (You might have looked at travel brochures in Book 1.)
>
> **Travel writing (sometimes called a travelogue)** text which describes someone's travels.

Telling the difference

1 Could you spot the difference between an extract from a brochure and an extract from a travelogue?

In pairs, look at these six mystery texts. Can you work out which ones are from holiday brochures and which are from travellers' accounts of their journeys?

For each text, pick out one phrase or sentence which best shows whether it is from a brochure or a piece of travel writing.

1 It's big, it's beautiful, it's impressive – and within this vast holiday area you'll find some glorious unspoilt sweeps of sand, breathtaking scenery, at least three national parks, and some of the most famous resorts in Britain. Scarborough, Whitby and Filey, and across the Pennines bouncy Blackpool with its tower, zoo and spectacular illuminations, and elegant Southport with its beautiful iron pier.

2 Overlooking the sheltered bay, the Gold Award-winning Hotel Queen's Bay offers beautiful views over the Paphian coast. Enjoy the comforts of this beautifully furnished hotel, where attractive sun terraces and gardens lead down to the shore. In a secluded setting, the Queen's Bay facilities allow pleasurable days to be spent either relaxing beside one of the two pools or participating in any of the activities on offer.

3 It really was like walking down the side of a house. And no one could stir a step without at least one arm round a tree. I had no gun to carry, so I clung frantically to each stem in succession.

4 6.40 am East 19th Street. The sound of ships' sirens comes booming up from the Hudson. Beaten-down-looking people, mostly old, are going to work now. The Empire State building is like a Roman candle in the sun which is roaring up over the East River.

5 Here in Haute Vienne the most successful industry is not farming but porcelain, relying on the many fine oxides which are found locally. The chief centre of the industry is Limoges, an old Roman city, which now boasts many craft shops and museums where you can both look and buy! The surrounding countryside is extremely pretty and home to many different events during the summer, whilst for excellent leisure facilities the lake at St Pardoux is hard to beat.

6 Surrounded by pretty gardens, the Uyal stands on the road leading directly to the resort centre. An excellent choice of cafés, bars and restaurants are within a 10 minute walk. A grand, older building houses the dining room and comfortable lounges, while the accommodation is in a more modern block. The friendly management and staff welcome back guests year after year.

2 How can we tell the difference between the two types of writing? The clues lie in the texts themselves, and in what they offer the reader.

From a holiday brochure, we probably want:

- information
- key facts about a place
- details which will help us to compare one holiday with another

From travel writing, we probably want:

- to learn about the writer's experiences
- to follow a storyline
- to be entertained

What other reasons for reading each type of text can you think of? Make a note of them.

3 What do we expect the written style of each type of text to be like – straightforward, descriptive, personal, impersonal, flowery?

Look at this list of words and sort them into two columns – one for travel brochures, one for travel writing. Some words might fit into both columns.

description
emotions
facts
people
places
prices
statistics
stories
memories
dialogue

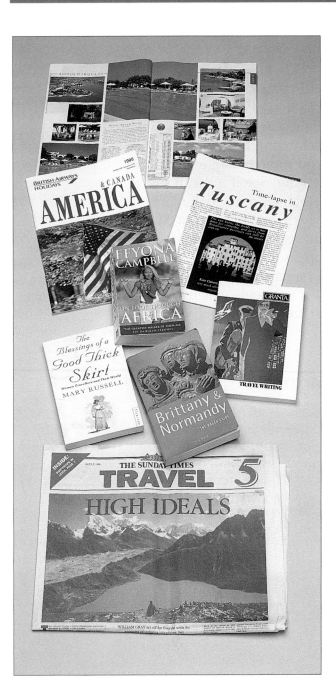

Travel brochures	Travel writing

Compare your choices with a friend's.

Looking at language

Now explore the language a little more deeply with this new challenge. The extract on the right contains some sentences belonging to holiday brochures and some belonging to travel writing. See if you can sort out which sentence belongs to which type of writing. As you untangle the sentences, be as precise as you can about the language clues which helped you to decide which type of writing they belong to.

Arrival in Spain

As we step off the plane the heat hits us powerfully (1). It is like stepping into a furnace, dressed in hat, coat and scarf (2). Temperatures at this time of year average out at around 85° (3). The bus from airport to hotel is a swift 45 minute transfer (4). Sitting on top of a steep hill, the hotel looks majestic and vaguely threatening (5). Inside, cool corridors and polite staff welcome weary guests (6). The pool is wonderfully refreshing (7). I swim for around an hour (8). Then I decide to explore the local town (9). Alicante is a place of history and tradition, well known for its lively atmosphere and giddy social life (10). The main shopping area is teeming with people and local musicians add to the excitement (11). Market traders are sweeping up after a long day's work (12). Back at the hotel, you can relax before dinner, sitting on the balcony and admiring the view (13). The hotel is renowned for its fine food (14). Dinner is served as the sun sets over the distant mountains (15).

A short visit to Sleeville

Sleeville is an industrial town near Royalby with a population of around 97,000 people. It is well-known for its steelworks and confectionery (sweets) manufacturing. The centre of the town has been pedestrianized, so that vehicles have no access except for loading and unloading. Much of the town was rebuilt in the 1960s after war damage. There are many major stores and good transport systems.

The Official Guide to Sleeville

This information gives you some facts about Sleeville. Imagine you are a traveller who has spent a day or so in the town. Try to bring it to life in a more imaginative way, giving the flavour of the centre of the town on a busy shopping-day.

You might mention:
- sights, sounds, smells
- people, buildings

You might use:
- description, dialogue
- this opening sentence: 'At the end of a lively day in Sleeville, I retired to my hotel and thought about what I had seen. It had all started at around 7 am …'

Write three or so paragraphs of detailed, descriptive writing.

The Ends of the Earth

Travel writing doesn't have to be about faraway places – for example, the writer Eric Newby has written about exploring a London department store, describing it as if it was a new country. Other writers describe scenes from their childhood as if they were foreign lands. But the most gripping travel writing takes us to places we will probably never see for ourselves.

Read these different descriptions of travels to the Antarctic, that vast, largely-unexplored continent at the bottom of the world. As you read the extracts, look for clues about the emotions the writers are feeling.

Roald Amundsen (1872-1928)

Amundsen was a Norwegian explorer and navigator, and the first human to reach both poles. He arrived at the South Pole on 14th December, 1911, thirty-five days before the British explorer, Captain Scott. Here he describes the moment of arrival …

At three in the afternoon a simultaneous 'Halt!' rang out from the drivers. They had carefully examined their sledge-meters, and they all showed the full distance – our Pole by reckoning. The goal was reached, the journey ended. I cannot say – though I know it would sound much more effective – that the object of my life was attained. That would be romancing rather too bare-facedly. I had better be honest and admit straight out that I have never known any man to be placed in such a diametrically opposite position to the goal of his desires as I was at that moment. The regions around the North Pole – well, yes, the North Pole itself – had attracted me from childhood, and here I was at the South Pole. Can anything more topsy-turvy be imagined?

We reckoned now that we were at the Pole. Of course, every one of us knew that we were not standing on the absolute spot; it would be an impossibility with the time and the instruments at our disposal to ascertain that exact spot. But we were so near it that the few miles which possibly separated us from it could not be of the slightest importance. It was our intention to make a circle round this camp, with a radius of twelve and a half miles (20 kilometres), and to be satisfied with that. After we had halted we collected and congratulated each other. We had good grounds for mutual respect in what had been achieved, and I think that was just the feeling that was expressed in the firm and powerful grasps of the fist that were exchanged. After this we proceeded to the greatest and most solemn act of the whole journey – the planting of our flag. Pride and affection shone in the five pairs of eyes that gazed upon the flag, as it unfurled itself with a sharp crack, and waved over the Pole.

Richard Evelyn Byrd (1888-1957)

Byrd was an American naval officer and explorer and one of the first humans to fly across the North Pole. Here he returns in a fierce blizzard to the hut in which he has spent four and a half months alone, on the Ross Ice Shelf. A new nightmare begins: he finds that he cannot open the entry latch …

Panic took me then, I must confess. Reason fled. I clawed at the three-foot square of timber like a madman. I beat on it with my fists, trying to shake the snow loose; and, when that did no good, I lay flat on my belly and pulled until my hands went weak from cold and weariness. Then I crooked my elbow, put my face down, and said over and over again, You damn fool, you damn fool. Here for weeks I had been defending myself against the danger of being penned inside the shack; instead, I was now locked out; and nothing could be worse, especially since I had only a wool parka and pants under my wind-proofs. Just two feet below was sanctuary – warmth, food, tools, all the means of survival. All these things were an arm's length away, but I was powerless to reach them…

…Half-frozen, I stabbed toward one of the ventilators, a few feet away. My mittens touched something round and cold. Cupping it in my hands, I pulled myself up. This was the outlet ventilator. Just why, I don't know – but instinct made me kneel and press my face against the opening. Nothing in the room was visible, but a dim patch of light illuminated the floor, and warmth rose up to my face. That steadied me.

Still kneeling, I turned my back to the blizzard and considered what might be done. I thought of breaking in the windows in the roof, but they lay two feet down in hard crust, and were reinforced with wire besides. If I only had something to dig with, I could break the crust and stamp the windows in with my feet. The pipe cupped between my hands supplied the first inspiration; maybe I could use that to dig with. It, too, was wedged tight; I pulled until my arms ached, without budging it; I had lost all track of time, and the despairing thought came to me that I was lost in a task without an end. Then I remembered the shovel. A week before, after levelling drift from the last light blow, I had stabbed a shovel handle up in the crust

somewhere to leeward. That shovel would save me. But how to find it in the avalanche of the blizzard?

I lay down and stretched out full length. Still holding the pipe, I thrashed around with my feet, but pummelled only empty air. Then I worked back to the hatch. The hard edges at the opening provided another grip, and again I stretched out and kicked. Again no luck. I dared not let go until I had something else familiar to cling to. My foot came up against the other ventilator pipe. I edged back to that, and from the new anchorage repeated the manoeuvre. This time my ankle struck something hard. When

I felt it and recognized the handle, I wanted to caress it.

Embracing this thrice-blessed tool, I inched back to the trap-door. The handle of the shovel was just small enough to pass under the little wooden bridge which served as a grip. I got both hands on the shovel and tried to wrench the door up; my strength was not enough, however. So I lay down flat on my belly and worked my shoulders under the shovel. Then I heaved, the door sprang open, and I rolled down the shaft. When I tumbled into the light and warmth of the room, I kept thinking, How wonderful, how perfectly wonderful.

Different responses

Discuss:

1 How do the two writers' emotions differ? Choose one word that you think best describes their feelings.

2 What picture do they give of the landscape of the Pole? Choose a sentence from each extract which you think gives the strongest impression of what the place is like.

3 The first text was written in 1911; the second in 1934. Find a word, phrase or sentence from each one that gives a clue about when it was written. Be ready to explain your choice.

Taking it further

1 What questions would you want to ask these explorers? Choose one of the writers and create an interview for a radio or television audience, in which they give an account of what happened to them and how they felt. Use words from the writers themselves in answer to your questions, where possible.

2 Richard Evelyn Byrd describes a moment of sheer panic, as he finds himself locked out of his shelter. Think of a time you have experienced panic and write an account of it. Here are some possible situations:

- suddenly thinking that you are lost
- being at home alone and thinking you heard something upstairs or outside
- realizing you have forgotten something vital

Choose a situation you have really experienced, and describe what happened from beginning to end. Try to give a strong sense of what panic feels like.

Language Study

The Changing Language

On page 94 you were given eight short magazine extracts and asked to decide which ones were from the 1990s and which from the 1930s.

A number of phrases might have caught your eye, simply because they are not used these days. For example, what would you say today instead of:

…there will come a time when it's just *too hopelessly short*…
Here's a little *catch*…
Unless she's *frightfully* bright…
…she'll be *stumped*…
'…heat does, you *silly*,…'

Changing slang

Slang is part of the very informal language that particular groups use in certain situations, sometimes to add vividness or humour. One area of slang which is constantly changing is the set of words which we use to describe things which are excellent. Here are some examples of those words taken from the seventeenth century to almost the present day.

1 In pairs, try to work out when some of these words were in use. For example, when did people describe things as 'ripping'?

2 When you have done that, add to the list any words of this kind which you and your friends currently use.

3 Finally, discuss as a class whether you all agree about which words are actually in use at the moment, which ones are the newest, and which are already out of date. Are you able to say what the origins of some of the most recent expressions are? (For example, 'fab' was simply an abbreviation of 'fabulous'.)

ripping	far-out	mega
A1	heavy	spiffing
cool	rich	bully
splendiferous	smashing	wicked
dandy	groovy	tip-top
classic	bad	awesome
ex	neat	brill
splendacious	sponditious	fab

Using Adjectives

Adjectives, as you will remember from Book 1, are words which give more information about nouns or pronouns.

Adjective families

It is sometimes helpful to think of adjectives as belonging to particular 'families', according to areas of meaning or use. For example, the publisher writing the memo to the marketing team on page 92 has selected adjectives from a 'family' which will give the impression that the proposed magazine will be original, fashionable and exciting.

Fill in the gaps below, either by remembering which adjectives were used in the memo, or by inventing new ones all from the same family.

```
This magazine is completely _____
and the readers are going to love
it! What's radically _____ is
that we're aiming to get teenagers
talking about fashion.

It will contain celebrities in
_____ clothing. It will
have fashion features. There will
be loads of _____ colour photos and
_____, _____ text.
```

Can you remember which adjectives the publisher used when trying to stress how good the advice would be? These are from a different family, giving the idea of being steady and practical.

Again, try to fill in the gaps with appropriate words:

```
...and give _____, _____ advice
on how to feel better about your
looks.
```

Compare your versions with the original on page 92.

Here is a list of adjectives from another extract in this module. What kind of family would you say they belonged to? Which words give you the greatest clue as to what the extract is about? To check, turn to page 110.

big	beautiful
impressive	vast
glorious	unspoilt
breathtaking	spectacular
elegant	

Adjectives can also be thought of as belonging to families of words which do not all have the same meaning but are used in the same context. A good example of this is the family of adjectives on page 98 describing different types of personalities, such as:

talkative	secretive
narrow-minded	tactful
imaginative	jealous

Look at the adjectives used in the first of the personal statements on page 97:

I am quite outgoing but at the same time a bit shy when I'm in the company of strangers. I like to have a laugh with people I know well. I'm enthusiastic about most things (usually) but I can become very moody.

Rewrite the passage, finding other adjectives which mean roughly the same, or at least give a similar impression. As you learned on page 78, these are known as **synonyms**.

117

More about Adverbs

In Book 1 you learned that adverbs tell us something about the verb in the sentence.
e.g. I *dug* [verb] *frantically* [adverb] at the snow...
The adverb 'frantically' tells us more about the verb 'dug'.

I dug frantically at the snow...

Adverbs can also tell us more about adjectives:
This magazine is *completely* [adverb] *new* [adjective]...
What's *radically* [adverb] *different* [adjective] is that...
I was *really* [adverb] *shy* [adjective] at first...

The most common adverb used in this way is *very*.

In pairs, look through the extracts in this book and find other examples of adverbs which tell us more about adjectives.

Looking at Sentences

One of the easiest things you can do with sentences in order to gain particular effects is to vary their type and length.

Varying the type of sentence you use

In Book 1 you learned that there were three kinds of sentence:

- a **simple sentence**, which says just one thing:
  e.g. Amundsen was a famous explorer.
- a **coordinated sentence**, which is what you get if you join two simple sentences with 'or', 'and', or 'but':
  e.g. Amundsen was a famous explorer *and* he beat Scott to the South Pole.
- a **complex sentence**, which uses a conjunction to show how the two parts of the sentence are joined in meaning:
  e.g. Amundsen was a famous explorer *because/after/when* he beat Scott to the South Pole.

Look back at two extracts in this module: the one about the origin of Coca-Cola (page 104); and Richard Evelyn Byrd's account of his experiences on the Ross Ice Shelf (pages 114–115).

What kinds of sentences are the ones which begin with the following words?

1 From *The Chronicle of Coca-Cola:*
'During the first year...' (l. 29)
'Dr Pemberton never realized...' (l. 32)
'He gradually sold portions...' (l. 33)

2 From Byrd:
'Then I remembered...' (l. 43)
'I lay down...' (l. 50)
'The hard edges at...' (l. 53)
'Then I heaved...' (l. 72)
'When I tumbled...' (l. 73)

Using shorter sentences

The Coca-Cola article is roughly 230 words long, the same length as the section of Byrd's account which begins, 'Then I remembered the shovel' and continues to the end.

Count the number of sentences in each of these extracts. What differences do you notice?

The two extracts have roughly the same proportion of simple, coordinated and complex sentences. But Byrd's sentences are very much shorter (on average, roughly half the length of the Coca-Cola writer's) and the effect is to give a great sense of tension, excitement and urgency to the writing.

Look at the two opening sentences, for example:

'Panic took me then, I must confess. Reason fled.' These sentences have tremendous impact because they are short, punchy and uncluttered.

Find another section in Byrd's writing where he puts three sentences together, each of under ten words long. Try to say what the particular effect is.

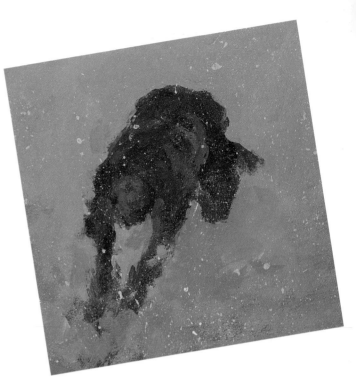

Combining longer and shorter sentences

Although many writers will advise you to keep sentences short as a rule, a writer can gain useful effects by mixing longer and shorter sentences. Look, for example, at the end of the second paragraph of the Coca-Cola article. The writer begins the paragraph ('Thinking that...') with three fairly long sentences to describe the attempts made to sell the new drink, and then concludes the paragraph with a short sentence:

'During the first year, sales averaged a modest nine drinks per day.'

1 Discuss in pairs what you think the effect of this is.

2 Now look at the final paragraph and discuss the effect of beginning with a short sentence and moving on to two longer ones.

Around the turn of the century, little-known actress Hilda Clark achieved lasting fame as the attractive consumer of Coca-Cola in an array of advertising materials distributed by the Company.

BIRTH OF A REFRESHING IDEA

The product that has given the world its best-known taste was born in Atlanta, Georgia, on May 8, 1886. Dr John Styth Pemberton, a local pharmacist, produced the syrup for Coca-Cola, according to legend, in a three-legged brass pot in his backyard. He carried a jug of the new product down the street to Jacobs' Pharmacy, where it was sampled, pronounced 'excellent' and placed on sale for five cents a glass as a soda fountain drink. Whether by design or accident, carbonated water was teamed with the new syrup to produce a drink that was at once 'Delicious and Refreshing', a theme that continues to echo today wherever Coca-Cola is enjoyed.

Thinking that 'the two Cs would look well in advertising', Dr Pemberton's partner and bookkeeper, Frank M. Robinson, suggested the name and penned the now famous trademark 'Coca-Cola' in his unique script. The first newspaper ad for Coca-Cola soon appeared in *The Atlanta Journal*, inviting thirsty citizens to try 'the new and popular soda fountain drink'. Hand-painted oilcloth signs reading 'Coca-Cola' appeared on store awnings, with the suggestion 'Drink' added to inform passers-by that the new beverage was for soda fountain refreshment. During the first year, sales averaged a modest nine drinks per day.

Dr Pemberton never realized the potential of the beverage he created. He gradually sold portions of his business to various partners and, just prior to his death in 1888, sold his remaining interest in Coca-Cola to Asa G. Candler. An Atlantan with great business acumen, Mr Candler proceeded to buy additional rights and acquire complete control.

Plays and the Gods

In this Drama module you will be thinking about two major questions:
1 Where have playwrights through the ages got their stories from?
2 What kinds of stages or acting spaces have performers used?

The twin search for stories and acting spaces has been going on for well over two thousand years, at least as far back as the Ancient Greeks…

Stories from Ancient Greece

Throughout the ages and right up to the present day, one of the greatest sources of stories has been the siege of Troy. Writers as far apart in time as the Greek Homer, William Shakespeare, and modern-day Tony Robinson have been fascinated by the rich array of characters involved, their heroic exploits, and their adventures on the journey home.

Researching the stories

1 Do some research in your library and then discuss in pairs what you know about:
   ■ what started the Trojan War
   ■ the death of Achilles
   ■ the Wooden Horse
   ■ Odysseus and the Cyclops
2 Now read the following story, which is about the Commander-in-Chief of the Greek forces, Agamemnon, and his wife, Queen Clytemnestra.

The Story of Agamemnon and Clytemnestra

When the Greek battle fleet was about to sail to Troy, they were delayed in harbour because there was no wind to fill their sails. King Agamemnon was impatient to leave and asked his High Priest to find out what could be done. His reply struck terror in the King…

The gods are angry, King Agamemnon. They will not give us the wind we need unless…

Unless what?

Unless you sacrifice your daughter, Iphigenia.

So be it. The gods must be satisfied.

So Agamemnon gave up his daughter to be sacrificed, and the Greeks got the wind they needed to sail to Troy. Ten years passed before the Greeks could defeat the Trojans and return home. But Agamemnon was not to receive the welcome that he had hoped for from his wife, Queen Clytemnestra, and his cousin, Aegisthus…

120

It has been ten long years, but you will soon be avenged, my daughter.

But to kill a king—

It is common justice that he should die, Aegisthus.

The gods will not see it that way.

Oh yes, they will.

Agamemnon has just won a great victory. He is a boastful man. If I can persuade him to claim all the glory of victory for himself and give none to the gods –

Of course! They will hate him for it –

And rejoice to see him punished for his pride and swaggering...

I shall lay a fine, red carpet...

If he so much as steps upon it before giving thanks to the gods...

...they will be enraged at his audacity. The killing will be an execution, not a murder.

I shall show him to his bath – he will be hot and dusty after his journey...

Then you and I will throw a great net over him, and the rest will be easy...

Staging the story

This powerful and violent story was a favourite one among the people of Ancient Greece. One writer who used it as a subject was the dramatist Aeschylus (pronounced *Ee-sker-luss*, with the stress on the first syllable).

In pairs, make a list of:

1 some of the difficulties that a dramatist might have in putting this story on stage

2 possible solutions to each of the difficulties that you have identified. For example:

■ The story covers a period of over eleven years and takes place in more than one country. How could you deal with those problems on stage?

■ How can you convincingly show a bloody bath-tub murder?

(Clue: what ways are there of letting the audience know that something has happened without actually showing it?)

When you have arrived at some solutions, read the extract on pages 122–123, to compare them with what Aeschylus actually did.

The Murder of Agamemnon

This is a modern version of part of Aeschylus's play. Agamemnon, having proudly walked on the red carpet, has entered the palace. Within seconds a group of a dozen citizens, standing outside the great wooden doors of the palace, hear Agamemnon's terrifying screams.

After Troy

1st citizen: That scream! She has killed him!

2nd citizen: Send a herald round – get all the citizens to get whatever weapons they can lay their hands on and meet here.

3rd citizen: Too slow. I say we break the doors down and catch her before the blood dries on the sword.

4th citizen: Yes. Act now.

5th citizen: We don't have to guess where this is leading. The killers are in power now and they'll rule like the bloody tyrants they are –

6th citizen: – While we stand around talking. In the name of the gods, let's do something.

7th citizen: But what? What can we do against them?

8th citizen: He's right. If the King's dead, we're not going to bring him back to life by making trouble.

9th citizen: What are we supposed to do, then? Live out the rest of our years with the stain of blood over our royal house?

10th citizen: I'd rather die! Better than living under tyrants.

11th citizen: Wait, though. What evidence have we got? A few screams? They could mean anything.

12th citizen: We can't act until we're sure. At the moment it's all pure guesswork –

(At this point all twelve start repeating their arguments, or some improvised version of them, until they build to a hubbub, interrupted by the palace doors opening, to reveal **Clytemnestra,** *her clothes spattered in blood, and, behind her,* **Agamemnon** *dead in a silver bath and wrapped in a great purple robe.)*

Clytemnestra: When I spoke to you before, I said what I decided you needed to hear. I will now unsay every word. What else was I to do but lie? You don't plan to kill your enemy by telling the world. Yes, this is my work and I'm proud of it. I caught him in a net, a

great fishing net, while he was bathing, washing off the deep-dyed dirt of the long voyage home. And I stabbed him. Twice. Twice he screamed. And as he lay there, I plunged my dagger in a third time and gave thanks to Zeus for answering my prayers, as Agamemnon belched out his life and showered me in drops of crimson rain. It was beautiful. Like a life-giving shower on a cornfield in spring. So this is how it is, my people of Argos.

Aeschylus
adapted by John O'Connor

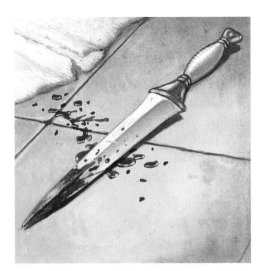

Staging the scene

1 Planning to act the scene
Form into groups of five and prepare a dramatized reading. How will you act

- the citizens? (Four of you will need to take three parts each.) Some are terrified, some angry; some impetuous, some reluctant.
- Clytemnestra? Do you sympathize with what she has done? What kind of person does she appear to be from this speech and her behaviour? How should she address the citizens? (Proudly? Uncertainly? Defiantly? Warily?)

2 Rehearsing the citizens
When you have done an initial reading, practise the citizens' speeches by reading them very urgently, trying to capture the excitement and terror of the moment. To do this, make sure that every speaker begins their speech before the previous speaker has quite finished. (This is known as 'cue-biting'.) When you reach the point where they all start repeating versions of their arguments, think up different speeches, but ones which are 'in tune' with your characters' earlier thoughts. Let this build to a confused hubbub.

3 Rehearsing Clytemnestra
Practise reading her speech so that you know it well. Which parts will you stress? What tone of voice will you use? How exactly will you interrupt the citizens and make yourself heard above their babble?

4 Rehearsing the movements
How will you stage the scene? Where should the citizens stand? How much should they move? Where does Clytemnestra enter from and what do the citizens do when she interrupts them? (For this performance, simply imagine the great doors and the dead Agamemnon.)

5 Performing the scene
When you have rehearsed, perform the scene to another group and discuss your acting decisions.

6 Aeschylus's stagecraft
Now that you have performed the scene, what would you say about the way in which Aeschylus has answered the difficulties of:

- showing an on-stage bloody murder?
- representing the terror of the population of Argos?

Looking at the way in which he uses the group of citizens here, how do you think he might have got round the problem of filling in the background details and showing what has happened in the years since Agamemnon left Argos to go to war?

The Greek Theatre

This is a photograph of the theatre at Epidauros in Greece. Built around 500 BC, it holds 20,000 people and is still used to stage plays by Aeschylus and the other dramatists from classical Greece. The building nestles in the hillside and is brilliantly designed. Stand at the very top and you can hear a coin drop on the centre spot.

The photograph below shows actors playing the citizens of Argos in the play about Agamemnon. Notice the masks that all the performers wore.

Researching the theatre of Ancient Greece

Use your library, as well as the photograph and illustration on this page to find out as much as you can about the ways in which plays were performed in the time of Aeschylus. For example:

1 On what special occasions were plays performed?
2 What do you know about the actors who took part?
3 What was the 'Chorus'? What was it for?
4 What part did masks play?

Oedipus and the Circle of Fate

Another favourite story was turned into three plays by a dramatist called Sophocles (pronounced *Soffer-cleese*). It is told in the diagram opposite. To read it, begin at Thebes…

Story into play

In pairs, try to answer the following questions and then compare your answers with another pair's.

1 Which scenes from the Oedipus story could easily be portrayed on the Greek stage?
2 Which ones would be very difficult to show?
3 Where would the play start and what would the Chorus or messenger have to relate?

Taking it further

Pick one scene that might be performable on the Greek stage and write it up in play form, involving a chorus to

■ set the scene
■ comment
■ be involved in the action

Finally perform it. If possible, you might try making your own simple masks.

OEDIPUS

CORINTH

THE CIRCLE OF FATE
THE RIDDLE OF THE SPHINX: what is it that goes on four legs in the morning, two in the afternoon, and three in the evening?

THEBES

He grows up to be Prince of Corinth.

But one day, visiting the Oracle at Delphi, his fate is revealed to him...

Horrified at the thought of harming the people he believes to be his parents, he runs away...

...and, in a fight on the road to Thebes, he kills a man. Unknown to him, this is his actual father, Laius, King of Thebes.

When Oedipus arrives in Thebes, the city is in the grip of the monstrous Sphinx. Oedipus saves them by answering its riddle, and...

...in their thanks, the people invite him to be King and marry their recently widowed Queen, Jocasta...

The shepherd takes the child to Corinth, where the King and Queen (who have no children) adopt him as their own and call him...

...where he is found by a shepherd working for King Polybus of Corinth.

So, when a boy child is born, Laius takes the baby and leaves it on a hillside to die...

King Laius of Thebes is told that, if he has a son, that son is fated to kill him and marry his mother.

FINISH — **DEATH** · **BIRTH** — **START**

125

Plays and the Bible

In the last unit you saw how the Greeks made plays out of the stories of their gods and goddesses, heroes and heroines. Throughout the world, people have always made plays based upon stories to do with their religion. Some of the best known stories in the western world are from the Bible.

Judas and the Great Betrayal

Judas: the story

1 What do you know about Judas? Brainstorm as a class all the details that you can remember.

2 Read the extracts from the Bible below, which recount the story of Judas's part in betraying Jesus.

The Bible

Jesus then came with his disciples to a place called Gethsemane. He said to them, 'Sit here while I go over there to pray.' ...Anguish and dismay came over him ... Then he came to the disciples and said to them, '...The hour has come! The Son of Man is betrayed to sinful men. Up, let us go forward; the traitor is upon us.'

While he was still speaking, Judas, one of the Twelve, appeared; with him was a great crowd armed with swords and cudgels, sent by the chief priests and the elders of the nation. The traitor gave them this sign: 'The one I kiss is your man; seize him;' and stepping forward at once, he said, 'Hail, Rabbi!', and kissed him. Jesus replied, 'Friend, do what you are here to do.' They then came forward, seized Jesus, and held him fast.

St Matthew's Gospel

Suddenly, while he was still speaking, Judas, one of the Twelve, appeared, and with him was a crowd armed with swords and cudgels, sent by the chief priests, lawyers, and elders. Now the traitor had agreed with them upon a signal: 'The one I kiss is your man; seize him and get him safely away.' When he reached the spot, he stepped forward at once and said to Jesus, 'Rabbi,' and kissed him. Then they seized him and held him fast.

St Mark's Gospel

While he was still speaking a crowd appeared with the man called Judas, one of the Twelve, at their head. He came up to Jesus to kiss him; but Jesus said, 'Judas, would you betray the Son of Man with a kiss?'

St Luke's Gospel

… There was a garden there, and he and his disciples went into it. The place was known to Judas, his betrayer, because Jesus had often met there with his disciples. So Judas took a detachment of soldiers, and police provided by the chief priests and Pharisees, equipped with lanterns, torches, and weapons, and made his way to the garden. Jesus, knowing all that was coming upon him, went out to them and asked, 'Who is it you want?' 'Jesus of Nazareth,' they answered. Jesus said, 'I am he.' And there stood Judas the traitor with them.

St John's Gospel

Selecting material

As you learned from your study of the Greek theatre in the last unit, when you decide to turn an episode from a written or spoken story into a play to be performed, you have to select the elements of the story which will be

- interesting to the audience
- possible to show on stage

Suppose you wished to perform this story in class or on a simple stage.

1 In pairs, make lists of
   - the most interesting elements of the story
   - the parts which would be difficult to show on a simple stage and the ways in which you might solve those difficulties

2 Plan what your play version of this episode might look like.
   - What would the main events be?
   - Is there any important background information to be conveyed in the dialogue?

- What decisions would you make about the main characters?
- What sort of language would you use? (For example, would you use verse or prose? Remind yourself of the choices by referring back to pages 144–145 of Book 1.)
- What, roughly, might the characters say to each other?

If you were planning to do a public performance:
- How would you deal with the setting?
- How would the characters dress?
- Would there be any props?

Improvising the scene

1 Form into groups of four and improvise a scene based upon Judas's betrayal, following as far as possible the decisions you have just made.

2 Watch other groups' versions and discuss the different ways in which the story was portrayed, according to the decisions that people had made.

Judas and the Mystery Plays

This is how the people of fifteenth-century York scripted the episode of Judas's betrayal. The version here is an updated one by the poet Tony Harrison, but it follows the original Middle English very closely. This extract also includes an earlier scene in which Judas makes the deal with Pilate. Read the scenes in groups of three.

The Mysteries

Scene 1

Judas: Sir Pilate most potent a plea I pursue
　　That Jesus, that Jew, I would sell unto you.
Pilate: What hightest thou?   [What are you called?]
Judas: Judas Scariot.
Pilate: Howgates bought shall he be?   [How shall he be bought?]
　　Bring forth thy bargain.
Judas: But for a little amends to bear hence again.   [For just a small payment to take away with me.]
Pilate: Nay, what shall we pay?
Judas: Sir, thirty pence flat; no more then.
　　I shall teach you a token him quick for to take   [I'll show you a sign…]
　　Where he is ringed in the throng; my word I will keep.
Pilate: We know him not.
Judas: Take care then that caitiff to catch   ['captive', slave]
　　Whom there I shall kiss…

Scene 2

Jesus: (*on his knees, praying*) Now in my flesh feared be,
　　　father, I am fain
　　That mine anguish and my noyes are near at an end.   [I want my torment and anxieties to come to an end.]

　(*He gets up.*)

　　Unto my disciples go will I again
　　Kindly to comfort them that mazed is in their mind.   [amazed]
　　Now will this hour be nighing full near   [getting very near]
　　That'll certify all the sooth that I've said.   [prove that all that I've said is true]

　(*Enter* **Judas**.)

Judas: All hail, Master, in faith, and fellows all here.
　　With great, gracious greeting on t'ground be arrayed.
　　I would ask you a kiss, Master, if your will it were,
　　For all my love and my liking wholly on you is laid.
Jesus: Full heartily, Judas, have it even here.

　(**Judas** *embraces* **Jesus**.)

　　For with this kiss is Man's Son betrayed.

Tony Harrison

Performing the play

1 In your group of three, rehearse the scenes, working out how the characters ought to be acted and what kinds of moves are required.

2 Compare your decisions with another group's.

Studying the text

Still in your groups of three, make notes on the following questions.

1 Are there any interesting parts of the Gospel accounts which the medieval playwrights chose not to use? Why do you think they left those out?

2 Look again at Scene 2.
   ■ Which parts of Jesus's and Judas's speeches seem not to have been taken from the Gospels? In other words, what do the playwrights seem to have invented?
   ■ How do these additions add to our interest in the two men as characters in a play?

Compare your responses to these questions with another group's.

Other scenes from the Mysteries

During the Middle Ages many other stories from the Bible were performed as plays, as you will learn on page 130. The photographs on this page are from a modern-dress performance of such plays.

The first one shows animals entering the ark. The story of Noah was one of the most popular, partly because of the excitement of the flood, partly because of the constant arguing between Noah and his wife! The second and third photographs show incidents from scenes which follow soon after the ones you have read.

Noah's Ark

Above: the Devil looks on in satisfaction while Jesus is maltreated before the crucifixion.

Right: Jesus on the cross, with Mary and others around him.

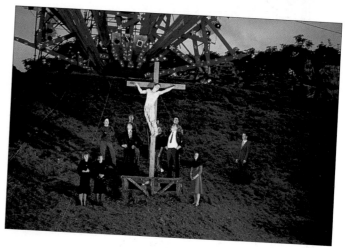

129

Mystery Plays

The story about Judas which you have just read was from a fifteenth-century 'Mystery Play'. Mystery plays contained stories which were mainly from the Bible and were performed by working people who belonged to craft guilds. (The word 'mystery' means a trade or craft.)

Watching a sequence of mystery plays was an experience in itself. You would stand in a good viewing place – say, the market square – and wait for a cart full of actors to arrive and perform the first play, possibly a story about God's creation of the world, on the cart itself (known as a pageant wagon). This first wagon would then leave and be replaced by a second, perhaps depicting the story of Adam and Eve, and then others throughout the day (and sometimes the following day), until the whole 'cycle' was completed. The wagons had two levels, with the actors using the curtained-off lower level as a changing room and the upper storey as an acting space.

Each guild would choose a story that fitted it. The Bakers might perform the Last Supper, for example, and the Shipwrights the story of Noah and the flood.

Changing the Audience

When the mystery plays were written, the creators had in mind a very varied audience of townspeople, young and old.

Writing for the primary school

1 In groups of four, discuss what decisions you would have to make if you were asked to write a version of the same Judas story for performance in your local primary school as part of an end-of-term event. For example, think about:

- the language
- the characters
- the events that you would choose to portray
- elements you might choose to miss out
- how you would stage the play

2 When you have made your decisions, try writing a draft of the first five or six speeches. As your 'raw material', use the ideas provided by both the four Gospels and the mystery play. But follow the example of the medieval playwrights: leave out whatever does not suit your purpose and add (within reason) whatever will make the story come alive on stage.

3 Rehearse your dialogue and perform it.

4 Discuss your play-writing choices and performance with other groups.

5 Finally, compare your versions with the one that follows, which was written for children in an Oxfordshire primary school.

Judas and the Great Betrayal

(*The set is completely empty except for Pilate's throne.*)

Scene 1

(**Pilate** *sitting on his throne,* **Cayaphas** *standing beside him; enter* **Judas**.)

Judas: Lord Pilate, all powerful, before you I kneel.
If it's Jesus you're after, I'll offer a deal:
Thirty pieces of silver's my bargain today –
Pilate: You lead me to Jesus and gladly I'll pay.
Cayaphas: But how shall we ken him, this 'King of the Jews'?
Amongst his disciples, which chap do we choose?
Judas: The one that you want won't be easy to miss:
You must go for the man that I greet with a kiss.
Pilate: You'd better be faithful and make good your claim.
Judas: Trust me… as Judas Iscariot's my name.

(**Judas**, **Pilate** *and* **Cayaphas** *freeze.*)

131

Scene 2

(**Jesus** *praying;* **disciples** *standing apart.*)

Jesus: I am so afraid, Father, for I know what is planned
And the hour of my torment is almost at hand.
My disciples are daunted and fearful of heart;
I must comfort them, Father, and then we must part.

(*He moves to them.*)

Now Peter and Andrew, Philip and John,
You must be of good cheer, let your worries be gone.

(*Enter* **Judas** *and* **soldiers**.)

For found is the friend we have come here to meet;
Our company's gathered. All is complete.
Judas: And this is my master, the man that I seek.
May I greet you, my lord, with a kiss on your cheek?
Jesus: Most heartily, Judas.

(**Judas** *kisses him.*)

Now the debt will be paid;
For with this one kiss mankind's Son is betrayed.

(**Jesus** *and the* **disciples** *freeze, as* **Judas** *moves across to* **Pilate**
and **Cayaphas**.)

Scene 3

Judas: I am suddenly stricken with conscience and guilt.
The kindness he showed me was candid and felt.
The master I sold you was loving to me:
You can take back your silver. Let him walk free!
Cayaphas: We've no interest, Judas, in your change of heart:
The bargain you bought was your plan from the start.
Pilate: We had an agreement and both of us win:
I have my 'Son of Man'. You have your sin.

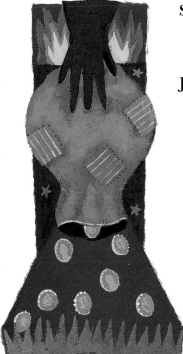

Scene 4

(*All the characters form a semi-circle behind* **Judas**, *who throws the money away and kneels.*)

Judas: My treacherous turn torments me with fire;
Now Judas forever is famed as a liar,
And ages to come will curse bitterly when
They spit the name Judas, betrayer of men.
This direst of deeds cannot undo nor mend,
I have no one to turn to, no brother nor friend;
My body I'll raise

(*he stands*)

but my soul must descend,
As mankind's beginning marks Judas's end.

(*The final line could be spoken by the whole cast.*)

John O'Connor

Looking at the staging

1 How successfully has the writer overcome the difficulty
of 'moving' from one scene to another?

2 How easy would it be for a group to perform this in
a classroom, without many props or any scenery?

Looking at the language

Four of the quotations which follow are from the Tony Harrison
version (based closely on the original mystery plays) and four
from the primary school version. Look carefully at the language
that the authors have chosen and discuss in pairs what all eight
extracts have in common.

- *Sir Pilate most potent*
- *Howgates bought shall he be?*
  Bring forth thy bargain.
- *take care then that caitiff to catch*
  whom there I shall kiss…
- *With great gracious greeting*
  on t'ground be arrayed.

- *But how shall we ken him,*
  this 'King of the Jews'?
- *My disciples are daunted*
  and fearful of heart;
- *And this is my master, the*
  man that I seek.
- *My treacherous turn*
  torments me with fire.

(As a clue, turn to page 74.)

Plays and History
Writing about a 'Real' Setting

Figures and events from history have been a popular source of play stories for centuries.

Sometimes a playwright bases a play upon real people who lived at a particular time in history. Shakespeare did this with many of his plays, including *Julius Caesar*, as you will see on pages 136–141.

At other times a playwright uses a real historical setting, but invents the characters, rather than portraying real people. This is what Richard Curtis and Ben Elton did with the fourth *Blackadder* series. The First World War background is real, but the characters are invented.

Blackadder and life in the trenches

1 Look at the still on this page, which is taken from an episode of *Blackadder Goes Forth*, and use it as a basis for a class brainstorm on what you know about the fighting conditions of the First World War. For example:

- What part did trenches play?
- What were dug-outs used for?
- What kinds of weapons were used?

2 Now read this extract, which features Captain Blackadder, Lieutenant George and Private Baldrick.

Blackadder Goes Forth

Blackadder: Baldrick, what are you doing out there?
Baldrick: (*off*) I'm carving something on this bullet, sir.

   (**Baldrick** *enters.*)

Blackadder: What are you carving?
Baldrick: I'm carving 'Baldrick', sir.
Blackadder: Why?
Baldrick: It's a cunning plan, actually.
Blackadder: Of course it is.
Baldrick: You see, you know they say that somewhere there's a bullet with your name on it…
Blackadder: Yes.
Baldrick: Well, I thought, if I owned the bullet with my name on it, I'd never get hit by it… 'Cos I won't shoot myself.
Blackadder: Oh, shame.

Baldrick: And the chances of there being two bullets with my name on them are very small indeed.

Blackadder: Yes. That's not the only thing around here that's very small indeed. Your brain, for example, is so minute, Baldrick, that if a hungry cannibal cracked your head open, there wouldn't be enough inside to cover a small water biscuit.

(**George** enters.)

George: Tally ho! Pip pip! And Bernard's your uncle!

Blackadder: In English we say 'Good morning'.

George: Look what I've got for you, sir.

Blackadder: What?

George: It's the latest issue of 'King and Country'. Oh, damned inspiring stuff: 'The magazine that tells the Tommies the truth about the war.'

Blackadder: Mmm…

Richard Curtis and Ben Elton

Background to the script

1 Baldrick's idea about having a bullet with his name on it refers to a common superstition of the war. What was it?

2 What sort of articles would you expect to find in George's magazine, 'King and Country'?

Describing the set

Write the stage directions to describe the set as it appears in the still photograph from the television series. The television designers have taken trouble to make it look as authentic as possible.

Looking at the characters

1 What does Baldrick's 'cunning plan' reveal about him?

2 What can you tell about George from the way he enters and from his enthusiasm for the magazine?

3 Look at the way Blackadder reacts to Baldrick's idea about the bullet and to George's greeting ('Tally ho!…'). What do these reactions reveal about the kind of person Blackadder is? What do you think he is likely to say about George's magazine?

Writing about 'Real' People

Often we do not know very much about historical figures as people – were they bad-tempered, for example, or lazy; untidy or generous? In cases like this, the dramatist has to invent quite a lot in order to make them interesting as characters in a play.

When Shakespeare wrote *Julius Caesar*, he had read about Caesar in the history books, but the character we see on stage also owes a great deal to Shakespeare's invention.

Shakespeare's play is about the death of the famous Roman leader and the bloody civil war which followed. The scene that you are about to read takes place on the steps of the Capitol – the Romans' Houses of Parliament. The streets are lined with crowds to cheer Caesar on his arrival. But among them is a group of men who are plotting to assassinate him: Brutus, Cassius, Casca, Decius, Metellus, Trebonius, and Cinna.

Caesar

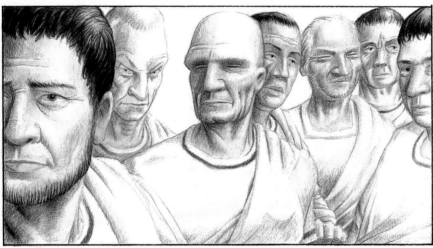
Brutus   Cassius   Casca   Decius   Metellus   Trebonius   Cinna

Soothsayer

Their plan is to stop Caesar outside the Capitol and, one by one, plead with him to allow Metellus's banished brother to return to Rome. They know that he will refuse, and they plan to use that as their cue to assassinate him.

Also among the crowds, however, are two men who are determined to warn Caesar if they can. One is a Soothsayer (or fortune-teller) who earlier warned Caesar to 'beware the ides [15th] of March'. The other is a citizen called Artemidorus, who has written a letter to Caesar (in the play called a 'schedule'), naming the men who are plotting against him…

Artemidorus

Acting the scene

Rehearse and act out the scene in groups of at least seven, then watch other people's versions.

Julius Caesar

Caesar: (*to the* **Soothsayer**) The ides of March are come.
Soothsayer: Ay, Caesar; but not gone.
Artemidorus: Hail, Caesar! Read this schedule.
Decius: Trebonius doth desire you to o'er-read,
   At your best leisure, this his humble suit.
Artemidorus: O Caesar, read mine first; for mine's a suit
   That touches Caesar nearer. Read it, great Caesar.
Caesar: What touches us ourself shall be last serv'd.
Artemidorus: Delay not, Caesar; read it instantly.
Caesar: What, is the fellow mad?
Publius: Sirrah, give place.
Caesar: What, urge you your petitions in the street?
   Come to the Capitol.

(**Caesar** *goes up to the Senate House, the rest following.*)

Popilius: I wish your enterprise today may thrive.
Cassius: What enterprise, Popilius?
Popilius: Fare you well.

(*Advances to* **Caesar**.)

Brutus: What said Popilius Lena?
Cassius: He wish'd today our enterprise might thrive.
   I fear our purpose is discovered.
Brutus: Look how he makes to Caesar: mark him.
Cassius: Casca, be sudden, for we fear prevention.
   Brutus, what shall be done? If this be known,
   Cassius or Caesar never shall turn back,
   For I will slay myself.
Brutus: Cassius, be constant.
   Popilius Lena speaks not of our purposes;
   For, look, he smiles, and Caesar doth not change.
Cassius: Trebonius knows his time; for, look you, Brutus,
   He draws Mark Antony out of the way.

(*Exeunt* **Antony** *and* **Trebonius**.)

Decius: Where is Metellus Cimber? Let him go,
   And presently prefer his suit to Caesar.
Brutus: He is address'd; press near and second him.
Cinna: Casca, you are the first that rears your hand.
Caesar: Are we all ready? What is now amiss,
   That Caesar and his Senate must redress?
Metellus: Most high, most mighty, and most puissant Caesar,
   Metellus Cimber throws before thy seat
   A humble heart, –

(*He kneels*.)

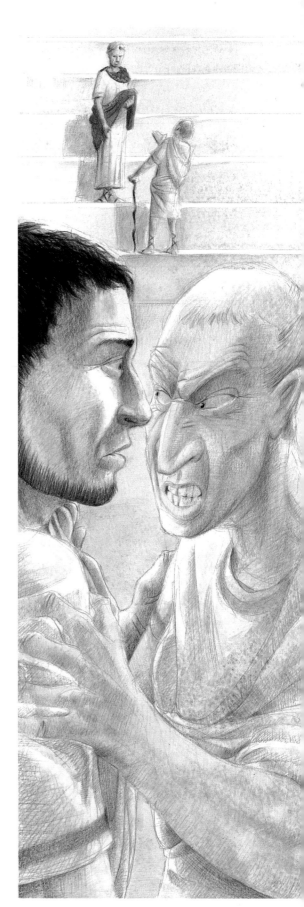

137

Caesar: I must prevent thee, Cimber.
These couchings and these lowly courtesies
Might fire the blood of ordinary men,
And turn pre-ordinance and first decree
Into the law of children. Be not fond
To think that Caesar bears such rebel blood
That will be thaw'd from the true quality
With that which melteth fools – I mean sweet words,
Low-crooked curtsies, and base spaniel fawning.
Thy brother by decree is banished;
If thou dost bend and pray and fawn for him,
I spurn thee like a cur out of my way.

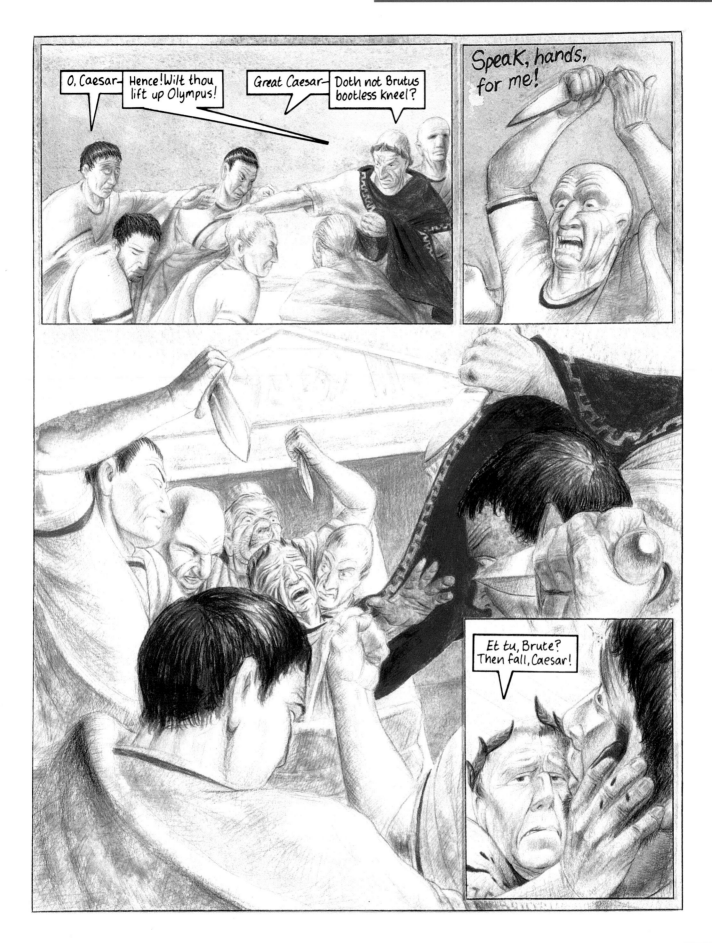

O, Caesar—

Hence! Wilt thou lift up Olympus!

Great Caesar—

Doth not Brutus bootless kneel?

Speak, hands, for me!

Et tu, Brute? Then fall, Caesar!

Liberty! Freedom! Tyranny is dead! Run hence, proclaim, cry it about the streets.

Some to the common pulpits, and cry out, 'Liberty, freedom, and enfranchisement!'

People and senators, be not affrighted; fly not; stand still; ambition's debt is paid.

Go to the pulpit, Brutus.

And Cassius too.

Where's Publius?

Here, quite confounded with this mutiny.

Stand fast together, lest some friend of Caesar's should chance—

Talk not of standing.

Publius, good cheer; there is no harm intended to your person, nor to no Roman else; so tell them, Publius.

Shakespeare's Sources

Shakespeare got many of his ideas about the characters in this play from a history book written by a Roman called Plutarch and translated in Shakespeare's day by Thomas North. This is what Plutarch wrote (in North's translation) about Caesar, Brutus, and Cassius:

Now Caesar immediately won many men's good wills in Rome, through his eloquence in pleading of their causes, and the people loved him marvellously also, because of the courteous manner he had to every man... But the chiefest cause that made him mortally hated was the covetous desire he had to be called king...

But Brutus... was a marvellous lowly and gentle person, noble-minded, and would never be in any rage... He could also plead very well in Latin...

But Cassius, being a choleric man, and hating Caesar privately more than he did the tyranny openly, he incensed Brutus against him.

GLOSSARY

eloquence	ability to speak well
courteous	polite, good-mannered
covetous	greedy
choleric	short-tempered
incensed	made him angry

In more detail

1. In pairs, list the details from Plutarch about each character that Shakespeare seems to have used. Has Shakespeare changed anything? For example:
   - Do you find Caesar 'courteous' here?
   - How did he come across when your group acted the part?
   - Did other groups portray him differently?

2. Look at the way the character of Caesar is acted in the version which appears on the video. How close is this Caesar to Plutarch's original description?

3. To gain an idea of how dramatic this scene is, imagine that you are a radio or television reporter doing a live commentary of Caesar's arrival at the Capitol. Work out what the reporter would say and perform the commentary, perhaps recording it. Remember that reporters often set the scene first (describing the weather, the crowds, particular figures they can identify) and then they go on to report what actually happens (describing people's actions and the crowd's reactions).

...Kate Marcus, News at X, the Capitol, Rome...

Shakespeare's Theatre

We don't know exactly what Shakespeare's theatre looked like, but we do have enough clues (for example, a drawing made at the time of a similar theatre by a Dutch visitor) to be reasonably sure about a number of important details. On this spread are printed some stills from the opening of Laurence Olivier's film *Henry V*, which also appears on the video, some photographs of the new replica of Shakespeare's Globe Theatre (which has been built in London very near the site of the original one) and the drawing by the Dutch visitor, Johannes de Witt.

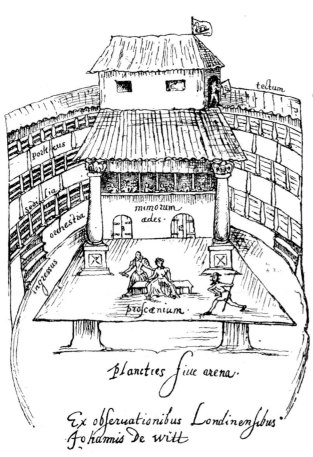

Reconstructing the Globe

1 Using these pictures and any other evidence from the *Henry V* sequence on video, list all the details you can about the appearance and atmosphere of Shakespeare's theatre. For example:

■ Roughly what shape was it, looked at from above?

■ How many storeys did it have?

■ Where was the stage in relation to the audience?

■ What was behind the stage?

■ Was there any scenery? Or lighting?

■ What was it like to be in the audience? What different kinds of view could you have?

Generally, what were the most striking differences between the Globe and most modern-day theatres?

2 Imagine that you are Johannes de Witt and have just visited the Globe for the first time. Write a letter (in English!) describing the theatre. Include a sketch. Don't simply copy de Witt's original (which was of a different theatre anyway), but use all the information that you have gathered from the photographs on these pages and from the video extract.

Plays and the Imagination
Monsters and Magic

Dramatists do not only get their ideas from stories about their religion or their history. Many of the best ideas spring from the imagination.

In each of the extracts that follow, the playwright has dug into his imagination to portray monstrous creatures or magical acts.

The Thwarting of Baron Bolligrew

The first extract is taken from a play by Robert Bolt. In it, the wicked Baron Bolligrew, assisted by his dim-witted sidekick, Squire Blackheart, and the cunning magician, Moloch, are plotting to get rid of the noble Sir Oblong Fitz-Oblong by feeding him to the Dragon. To do this, they have put Oblong under a magic spell called Grimbleboots.

Presenting the Dragon

1 Before you read the extract, discuss in pairs how Bolt might have decided to represent the Dragon (who has to hold a conversation with the other characters). Since it is not possible to bring a dragon on stage (he is described as 'bigger than four carthorses'), what else can you do?

2 In a group of five, read this extract aloud. A Storyteller sets the scene…

The Thwarting of Baron Bolligrew

Storyteller: The Dragon lived in a black and silent valley which had once been green with pasture. His den looked like a railway tunnel without any signals or track.

(*Black backdrop descends to cover church, with black archway in it.*)

Those who had seen him, by moonlight, knew that he was bigger than four carthorses, and sleek, and black, and shiny. Like all black dragons he seldom came out except at night, because his eyes were weak. And in the day, these eyes were all that could be seen of him.

(*Red eyes switched on in blackness of arch.*)

And all that could be heard of him was an occasional roar –

(**Dragon** *roars on Speaker.*)

And an occasional complaint; for the Dragon was always discontented, and talked to himself continually.

Dragon: (*on Speaker throughout*) I'm bored… There's no avoiding it; I'm thoroughly bored…

Blackheart: Look 'ere, Bolligrew. You see I've just remembered a pressin' engagement.

Bolligrew: Well forget it again.

(*He draws upstage towards the tunnel. Exit* **Storyteller** *simultaneously.*)

Hello…? Afternoon…! Anyone at 'ome?

Dragon: Do I hear the voice of a human bean?

(*On Speaker, noise between that of approaching train and cantering horse; eyes growing larger.*)

Bolligrew: It's me! Bolligrew!

(*Clatter of hooves, squeal of brakes. Hiss. Smoke curls from tunnel roof.*)

Dragon: Oh… Bolligrew… Is that Moloch?

Bolligrew: Dragon, we're a bit pressed for time. This proposal of yours for takin' over half of my half of the Island –

Dragon: – Yes?

Bolligrew: Seems quite reasonable to me.

Dragon: It does?… That's odd… Baron, there are no *strings* attached to this, are there?

Bolligrew: (*reels out of* **Dragon***'s sight, mopping brow with handkerchief. Shakily*) Strings, old chap? Don't know what you mean!

Dragon: Moloch. *You* haven't anything up your smelly old sleeve, have you?

Moloch: A reasonable suspicion, Dragon, but the answer happens to be 'no'. There's something we want you to do.

Dragon: That's better. What?

Bolligrew: Well it's about this feller Oblong. I don't know if you've heard –

Dragon: I have heard, yes.

Bolligrew: Well we were wonderin', if he 'appened to come wanderin' over 'ere, if you might like to, er, well – nosh 'im!

Dragon: But Baron, people *don't* wander over here.

Moloch: He will, Dragon, he will. We are using Grimbleboots. He will come very quietly – if you wish it, *without* his sword.

Dragon: Understand. Is he a good man?

Moloch: All the way through I think. I shall be interested to hear.

Dragon: Well. That's worth waiting for.

Moloch: Tomorrow then, at three o'clock?

Dragon: Tomorrow at three.

Bolligrew: There we are then! Good-bye old chap!

Dragon: Good-bye Baron, good-bye…

(*Eye-lights off.*)

Robert Bolt

Working on voices

1 Still in your group, discuss the following points.

- When you read the extract, what kind of voice did your Dragon have? Bolt himself suggested that it should sound 'languorous [lazy], upper-class, sinister', while the Storyteller adds that the Dragon was 'always discontented'.
- Blackheart is described as 'huge and stupid'. Think back to your reading: was this reflected in his voice? How could you achieve this effect?
- What about Bolligrew and Moloch? Although both 'bad' characters, they are very different in other ways. Moloch is Professor of Wickedness at Oxford, for example! Did their voices sound different? How could you ensure that they do?

2 Try different voices that will fit these qualities and then perform the extract again.

A radio play

Although the sight of the Dragon's red eyes in the blackness can be very impressive in the theatre, this is also a scene which comes alive on radio, where the listeners can imagine the monster and its lair. Act out a radio performance and record it on a cassette recorder. If you can, make or find some sound effects to represent the approach of the Dragon. Finally, listen to other groups' versions and compare such features as characters' voices and sound effects.

The Tempest

Shakespeare's play *The Tempest* is set on an island where the only inhabitants are Prospero (a magician), his daughter Miranda, a spirit called Ariel, and a monstrous creature known as Caliban, the son of a witch. In this scene, Caliban curses Miranda and Prospero, and the magician retaliates by listing all the torments that will be inflicted upon the monster.

The Tempest

(*Enter* **Caliban**.)

Caliban: As wicked dew as e'er my mother brush'd
With raven's feather from unwholesome fen
Drop on you both! a south-west blow on ye,
And blister you all o'er!

Prospero: For this, be sure, to-night thou shalt have cramps,
Side-stitches that shall pen thy breath up: urchins
Shall for that vast of night that they may work
All exercise on thee: thou shalt be pinch'd
As thick as honeycomb, each pinch more stinging
Than bees that made 'em.
Caliban: I must eat my dinner.
This island's mine, by Sycorax my mother,
Which thou tak'st from me. When thou camest first,
Thou strok'dst me, and made much of me; wouldst give me
Water with berries in't; and teach me how
To name the bigger light, and how the less,
That burn by day and night: and then I lov'd thee
And show'd thee all the qualities o' th' isle,
The fresh springs, brine-pits, barren place, and fertile.
Cursed be I that did so! – All the charms
Of Sycorax, toads, beetles, bats, light on you!
For I am all the subjects that you have,
Which first was mine own king; and here you sty me
In this hard rock, whiles you do keep from me
The rest o' th' island.

William Shakespeare

Curses and complaints

1 In pairs, read the passage carefully again
and list:
- the different curses that Caliban hopes
will fall on Prospero
- the punishments that Prospero intends
to inflict upon Caliban
- Caliban's complaints against Prospero

2 Discuss whether it is possible to feel
sympathetic towards Caliban after reading
this exchange.

The playwright and the monster

1 Shakespeare never really describes
Caliban, except that the monster himself
talks about his 'long nails' and other
characters call him 'half a fish and half a
monster', and say that he is not of human
shape. How do you imagine him? Does he
remind you of monsters from science
fiction films that you have seen, for
example? Which of the versions pictured
here comes nearest to your impression?

2 Write a brief description of each of the
Calibans pictured here as though you
were writing stage directions ('Caliban
has a slimy skin…'); then write stage
directions to describe your idea of the
perfect Caliban.

Red Dwarf

All is calm on the space mining vessel *Red Dwarf* until Holly, the ship's computer, suddenly issues a dramatic warning to one of the crew, Arnold Rimmer...

Red Dwarf: Polymorph

Holly: I don't want you to panic, Arn, but it does appear there's a very tiny possibility that there may very well in all likelihood possibly be a non-human life form on board.

Rimmer: You mean like last time? When you got us all worked up and we went scooting off down to the cargo bay, complete with bazookoids and backpacks and it turned out to be one of Lister's socks!

Holly: I didn't recognize the genetic structure. Biologically speaking they were a completely new life form.

Rimmer: Absolutely ridiculous! I felt a total goit.

Holly: Well, I think you should take a butcher's.

Rimmer: (*Impatiently*) Where is it?

Holly: I lost it. It's somewhere along the habitation decks.

Rimmer: (*Mutters*) Can't get a moment's peace!

(**Rimmer** *gets up angrily and leaves the room.*)

Rimmer goes off in search of the creature but is unable to prevent it attacking Lister, his crew-mate, who is then attended to by Kryten, the ship's robot, and the Cat (a life form evolved from the ship's pet)...

Cat: (*Concerned*) Is he OK?

Rimmer: As far as we can tell, yes.

Cat: So where'd the creature go?

Rimmer: (*Doubtful*) Well, it turned into a sort of splodgy, squelchy thing and squidged off down the corridor.

Cat: What is it? Some form of alien?

Holly: No, it's from Earth. Man-made. I checked out its DNA profile. Some kind of genetic experiment that went wrong.

Kryten: Apparently it was an attempt to create the ultimate warrior: a mutant that could change shape to fit its terrain and deceive its enemies.

Cat: So what did go wrong?

Kryten: (*As though from a horror movie*) It's insane!
Holly: It feeds off your negative emotions – fear, guilt, anger, paranoia – drains them out of its prey.
Kryten: It's a sort of emotional vampire. It changes shape to provoke a negative emotion. In Lister's case it took him to the very limit of his terror and then sucked out his fear.
Rimmer: So now Lister's got no fear?
Kryten: Precisely.
Rimmer: What are we gonna do?

Rob Grant and Doug Naylor

Stage directions not original – substituted by John O'Connor

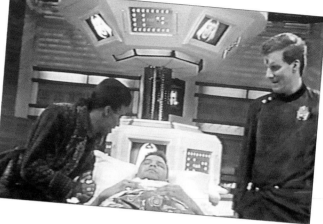

What is going to happen?

At this point Lister wakes up. Discuss as a class what you think his reaction to the situation is going to be now that he has no fear. (If you already know the story, listen to others' ideas before explaining what actually happens.)

Storyboarding the polymorph

Because the creature can change its shape, it is called a 'polymorph' (from two Ancient Greek words meaning 'many' and 'shape'). In one scene in this story it turns itself from a bouncing ball, to a sausage on Lister's plate, to a pair of his boxer shorts (which he puts on) and then, after Kryten has thrown the 'shorts' away, into an enormous snake!

Storyboard a short sequence in which a polymorph gets into your house or classroom (or any other inconvenient place).

Remember that the first few things that the creature turns itself into should be ordinary and not noticeable. You might even pick it up or use it. But the final one in the sequence is designed to have a powerful effect on the victim, so that it can suck the emotion out. For example, it should be something very scary if it wants to suck out the emotion of fear, or it might be a pile of money if the emotion is greed, or something really irritating if it wants the emotion to be anger.

Your teacher will give you advice on storyboarding.

'Red Dwarf' on video

Look again at the *Red Dwarf* sequence on the video. Study the different ways in which each character behaves (including Holly) and discuss as a class what you can tell about the kinds of people they are. (For example, are they bad-tempered, gloomy, intelligent…?) If you have watched the series on television, comment on how typical each character's behaviour is here.

Language Study

Middle English

On pages 80–81 you learned about Old English, the language spoken by the Anglo-Saxons. The play about Judas on pages 128–129 and the poem about blacksmiths on page 73 were both originally written in a version of the language which we call **Middle English**. This was spoken from around the twelfth to the fifteenth centuries.

This is the first half of the poem about Blacksmiths as it originally looked in Middle English. A word-for-word translation has been printed under each line.

Blacksmiths

Swarte smekyd smethes smateryd wyth smoke
Swarthy smoked smiths, smudged with smoke
Dryve me to deth wyth den of here dyntes.
Drive me to death with din of their strokes.
Swech noys on nyghtes ne herd man never:
Such noise on nights (not) heard man never:
What knavene cry and clateryng of knockes!
What knaves' cry and clattering of knocks!
The cammede kongons cryen after 'col, col!'
The crook-nosed monsters cry after 'Coal! Coal!'
And blowen here bellewys, that al here brayn brestes:
And blow their bellows, that all their brain bursts:
'Huf, puf!' seith that on; 'haf, paf!' that other.
'Huff, puff!' says the one, 'Haff, paff!' says the other.
Thei spyttyn and spraulyn and spellyn many spelles;
They spit and sprawl and tell many stories;
Thei gnaven and gnacchen, thei gronys togydere,
They grind and gnash their teeth, they groan together,
And holdyn hem hote wyth here hard hamers.
And make themselves hot with their hard hammers.

Anon., trans. John O'Connor

Changing language

In pairs, discuss how much the language has changed since this was written in the early 1400s.

1 How many words have remained exactly the same?
2 How many are not exactly the same, but are easily recognizable?
3 How many words seem to have disappeared altogether?

150

Chaucer and the Canterbury Tales

The most famous English writer from the Middle Ages is Geoffrey Chaucer, whose best known work is *The Canterbury Tales*. In this long poem, Chaucer tells of a group of pilgrims who are making the journey from London to Canterbury, to visit the tomb of Saint Thomas Becket. Chaucer first describes each of the pilgrims – there are roughly 30 in all.

Then the owner of the inn where they are staying suggests a contest: the pilgrims are to tell stories to pass the time on the journey and the teller of the best one will get a free meal when they return.

Introducing the pilgrims

Here are some of the pilgrims, with extracts from Chaucer's descriptions of them. Use the illustrations and footnotes to help you translate the extracts.

The Canterbury Tales

The Squire is the Knight's son, fashion-conscious and pleasure-seeking:

> Embrouded[1] was he, as it were a meede[2]
> Al ful of fresshe floures, whyte and reede.
> Syngynge he was, or floytynge[3], al the day;
> He was as fressh as is the month of May.
> Short was his gowne, with sleves longe and wyde.

Notes: [1]embroidered; [2]meadow; [3]playing the flute

The Yeoman is a keeper on the Knight's estate:

> And he was clad in cote and hood of grene.
> A sheef of pecok arwes, bright and kene,
> Under his belt he bar ful thriftily[1]…
> And in his hand he baar a myghty bowe.

Notes: [1]very handily

The Monk loves hunting and eats well:

> His heed was balled, that shoon as any glas,
> And eek[1] his face, as he hadde been enoynt[2].
> He was a lord ful fat and in good poynt[3];
> His eyen stepe[4], and rollynge in his heed,
> That stemed as a forneys of a leed[5];
> His bootes souple, his hors in greet estaat[6].

Notes: [1]also; [2]anointed; [3]in good shape; [4]glaring; [5]gleamed like the fire under a cauldron; [6]in fine condition

The Shipman is from Dartmouth in Devon:
> He rood upon a rouncy, as he kouthe [1],
> In a gowne of faldyng [2] to the knee.
> A daggere hangynge on a laas [3] hadde he
> Aboute his nekke, under his arm adoun.
> The hoote somer hadde maad his hewe [4] al broun…

Notes: [1]He rode upon a heavy horse, as well as he could; [2]coarse cloth; [3]cord; [4]colour

The Wife of Bath has had five husbands and is looking for a sixth:
> Gat-tothed was she, soothly [1] for to seye…
> Ywympled wel [2], and on hir heed an hat
> As brood as is a bokeler or a targe [3];
> A foot-mantel [4] aboute hir hipes large,
> And on hir feet a paire of spores sharpe.

Notes: [1]She had gaps between her teeth, truly…; [2]wearing a fine head-dress; [3]small or light shield; [4]overskirt down to her feet (to wear when riding)

The Miller is an expert wrestler:
> Upon the cop [1] right of his nose he hade
> A werte [2], and theron stood a toft of herys,
> Reed as the brustles of a sowes erys [3];
> His nosethirles [4] blake were and wyde.
> A swerd and bokeler [5] bar he by his syde.
> His mouth as greet was as a greet forneys [6]…

Notes: [1]tip; [2]wart; [3]red as the bristles of a sow's ears; [4]nostrils; [5]small shield; [6]furnace

The Reeve was a very unpopular official on the estate:
> The Reve was a sclendre colerik man [1].
> His berd was shave as ny [2] as ever he kan;
> His heer was by his erys ful round yshorn [3];…
> Ful longe were his legges and ful lene,
> Ylyk [4] a staf; ther was no calf ysene [5].

Notes: [1]thin, bad-tempered man; [2]closely; [3]cut round; [4]like; [5]to be seen

The Pardoner sold fake holy relics:
> This Pardoner hadde heer as yelow as wex,
> But smothe it heeng as dooth a strike of flex [1];
> By ounces [2] henge his lokkes that he hadde,
> And therwith he his shuldres overspradde;
> But thynne it lay, by colpons [3] oon and oon.

Notes: [1]bunch of flax; [2]shreds; [3]bundles (rats' tails)

Geoffrey Chaucer

Prefixes

When the writers of *Red Dwarf* decided that their monster should be called a Polymorph, they were using their knowledge of two word elements which come from Ancient Greek: *Poly-* (meaning 'many') and *-morph* (meaning 'shape').

Many English words have been formed in exactly this way, by taking 'building-blocks' from Latin and Greek.

When these elements come at the beginning of a word, they are called **prefixes**. Some of the most common are the ones we use to turn a word into its opposite (such as likely – *un*likely). How many different 'negative prefixes' can you find in the following words? Form groups of words which have the same prefix.

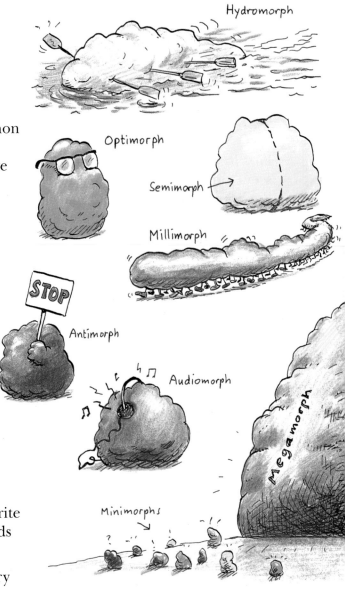

disappear	disappoint
irrelevant	inexpensive
dissatisfied	dishonest
illegal	illegible
disagree	impolite
irregular	impatient
immortal	disobedient
illiterate	inaccurate
impure	irreligious
unkind	incapable
inconvenient	undo
incorrect	

Which spelling rules can you state, to help people to write these negative words correctly? (Look especially at words such as appear – *dis*appear.)

Here are some other common prefixes. Use a dictionary to check what each one means, if you are not sure, and then write down an example of a word in which it is found, with its meaning.

anti	inter	multi	pre
auto	micro	photo	re
bio	milli	poly	sub
cent	mono	post	trans

Returning to Play Script, Dialogue, and Reported Speech

In Book 1 you learned how to set out a play script and how to punctuate dialogue correctly. On page 42 of Book 2 you were introduced to the idea of reported speech.

The extracts on these pages will help you to revise what you know about these three different ways in which to write down what people say.

The layout of play scripts

First look at this extract from the *Red Dwarf* scene on pages 148–149 and, in pairs, discuss the notes surrounding it to make sure that you understand all about how to set out play script dialogue:

The character's name is printed on the left-hand side before each speech.

You do not need speech marks.

Playscripts often use a colon after the name, to show that something is to follow.

Holly: Well, I think you should take a butcher's.
Rimmer: (*Impatiently*) Where is it?
Holly: I lost it. It's somewhere along the habitation decks.
Rimmer: (*Muttering*) Can't get a moment's peace!

(*He gets up angrily and leaves the room.*)

Stage directions show the things that are happening which are important to the story, or how a character is saying something or behaving.

Now redraft this next sequence (trying to remember who said what!) so that it is clearly set out. When you have finished, you can check your version with the original on page 148.

Is he OK? As far as we can tell, yes. So where'd the creature go? Well, it turned into a sort of splodgy, squelchy thing and squidged off down the corridor. What is it? Some form of alien? No, it's from Earth. Man-made. I checked out its DNA profile. Some kind of genetic experiment that went wrong.

154

The punctuation of dialogue

If the extract from *Red Dwarf* were to be rewritten as part of a novel or short story, it would look something like this. Again, check in pairs that you are familiar with the rules for punctuating dialogue:

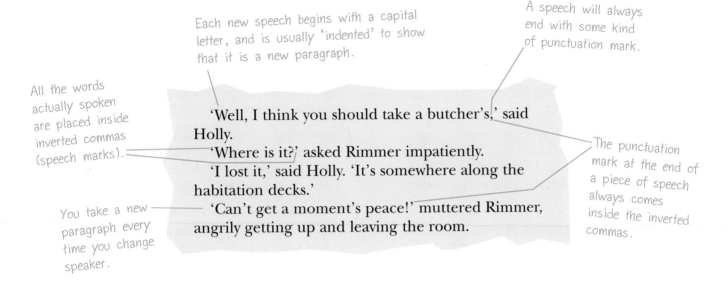

Each new speech begins with a capital letter, and is usually 'indented' to show that it is a new paragraph.

A speech will always end with some kind of punctuation mark.

All the words actually spoken are placed inside inverted commas (speech marks).

The punctuation mark at the end of a piece of speech always comes inside the inverted commas.

You take a new paragraph every time you change speaker.

'Well, I think you should take a butcher's,' said Holly.
'Where is it?' asked Rimmer impatiently.
'I lost it,' said Holly. 'It's somewhere along the habitation decks.'
'Can't get a moment's peace!' muttered Rimmer, angrily getting up and leaving the room.

Turning dialogue (direct speech) into reported speech

The notes surrounding this next extract point out some of the steps that have to be taken when you turn a piece of direct speech into reported speech.

It will usually be necessary to add 'that'.

The first and second person pronouns (I, we, and you) change to the third person pronouns (he, she, it, or they).

Slang expressions have to be placed inside quotation marks.

Verbs are usually 'shifted back' a tense so that they change from present to past.

Holly said that she really did think that Rimmer should 'take a butcher's'. Rimmer asked impatiently where it was. Holly replied that she had lost it, but that it was somewhere along the habitation decks. Rimmer muttered that he could not get a moment's peace, got up angrily and left the room.

Look again at the dialogue which follows this exchange (from 'Is he O.K.?' to '... that went wrong.') and, in pairs, rewrite it,

1 as direct speech in a novel
2 as reported speech

GLOSSARY

Abstract noun   The label given to something you cannot touch, such as an emotion, feeling or idea, e.g. hunger, boredom, skill. See page 43.

Accent   The way we pronounce words. Our accent usually depends upon where we were brought up, or the people we have spent most time with.

Adjective   A word which helps to give more information about a noun or pronoun, e.g. The *sunny, slow, lulling* afternoon yawns … It's *unbelievable*. See page 117.

Adverb   A word which gives us more information about a verb, e.g. Ruth went to look into it and drew back *quickly* … Those to work in the fields are *always* tired. See page 118.

Alliteration   The repetition of consonant sounds in order to gain a special effect, e.g. *B*low their *b*ellows till their *b*rains *b*urst. See page 74.

Apostrophe   The punctuation mark (') which has two quite different uses:
1   to show that a letter or group of letters has been missed out, e.g. It*'s* just too much. I*'ll* do it. We*'ve* finished.
2   to show possession (or ownership), e.g. *Zlata's* Diary, *Nightjohn's* smile.

Audience   The name we give to the people we expect to read our writing or listen to what we say. It can also mean the people who watch a play or film.

Autobiography   See **Biography**

Ballad   A poem which tells a story and is written in a particular form. See pages 48–51.

Biography and **Autobiography**   A biography is a book or article written about somebody's life. In an autobiography you write about *your own* life.

Borrowing   The English language has grown by borrowing words from other languages, e.g. *tea* comes from Chinese. See also **Etymology**.

Character   A person in a story, play, or poem.

Collective noun   The label we give to groups or collections of people, things, or animals, e.g. *crowd, sheaf, flock*. See page 43.

Comma   A punctuation mark (,) used to break up sentences and make them easier to understand, for example by separating items in a list or dividing up the different parts of the sentence.

Common noun   The general label we give to people, things, or animals, e.g. vicar, coconut, horse. See page 42; also **Noun**.

Conjunction   A word used to join parts of a sentence, individual words, or phrases, e.g. He waited *until* she had finished reading. She closed the book *and* put it down.

Consonant   The sound we make by using parts of the mouth to stop the air briefly, e.g. the first sounds in *cat, dog, bird*. See also **Alliteration**.

Coordinated sentence   See **Sentence**.

Dialect   A variety of language used by a particular group of people, which has its own words and expressions and its own set of grammatical rules. See also **Standard English** dialect.

Dialogue   Characters' spoken words in a story. See pages 154–155.

Direct speech   A speaker's exact words reproduced in writing, usually with speech punctuation, e.g. 'My name is Lee!' I almost yelled. See page 155.

Etymology   An account of the history of a particular word, including the language it came from and its original meaning, e.g. the etymology of 'biography' is two Ancient Greek words meaning 'life' and 'writing'.

Exclamation mark   The punctuation mark (!) used to end a sentence or a speech in a piece of dialogue if we want to show, for example, that a command has been given or something has been said urgently, e.g. 'Open it!' 'It's locked!'

Fiction   Writing which is about people and events which have been invented by the author, e.g. novels, such as *Fireweed*, and short stories, such as *The Call*.

Form   The kind of writing we are reading or producing, e.g. letter, poem, advertising leaflet.

Full stop   A punctuation mark (.) used to show the end of a sentence which is usually a statement, rather than a question or exclamation.

Grammar   The way words are put together or changed to make sentences. *Grammar* can also mean the 'rules' of a language or dialect.

Haiku   A special kind of poem from Japan, which usually has an image or picture, and is written in a particular number of syllables. See page 65.

Inverted commas   The punctuation marks ('...'). These are sometimes called quotation marks or speech marks and are used in the punctuation of speech. See pages 42, 154–155.

Limerick   A funny poem which usually tells a short story and is written in a particular form. See pages 44–45.

Metaphor   A way of comparing two or more things without using the words 'like' or 'as', e.g. Rockets and Roman candles make an orchard of the sky. See page 58.

Middle English   The name given to the English language as it was from around the twelfth to the fifteenth centuries. See pages 150–152.

Mystery Play   A play performed in the Middle Ages, based on a story from the Bible. See page 130.

Narrative   Writing or speaking which tells a story.

Non-fiction   Writing which is not stories, poems or plays, but deals mostly in facts, e.g. recipes, holiday brochures, encyclopedia articles. See Module 3.

Noun   The word in a sentence which labels a person, place, thing, feeling, or idea, e.g. It was on a dreary *night* of *November* that I beheld the *accomplishment* of my *toils*. Nouns can be **singular**, e.g. The *snake* raises its *head*. Or they can be **plural**, e.g. The *snakes* raise their *heads*. See pages 42–43; also **Proper noun**, **Common noun**, **Abstract noun**, and **Collective noun**.

Old English   The name given to the earliest form of English, spoken by the people who came to these islands in the fifth century. It is sometimes called Anglo-Saxon. See page 80.

Onomatopoeia   A word or phrase whose sound gives a kind of echo of its meaning, e.g. *mumbled* and *muttered*. See page 70.

Paragraph   A block of sentences linked by one overall idea or topic, e.g. the first paragraph of the extract by Roald Amundsen on page 113 contains eight sentences, all about the explorer's arrival at the South Pole and his feelings about getting there.

Parts of speech   See **Word class**.

Person   See **Verb**.

Personification   A special kind of **metaphor** in which an object or idea is described as though it were a person, e.g. Forest could keep secrets. See page 60.

Plot   The series of events in a story and the way they are linked together.

Plural   See **Noun**.

Prefix   A group of letters which we add to the beginnings of words to change their meanings, e.g. *poly-* (many), *anti-* (against), and *pre-* (before). See page 153.

Pronoun   A word which can be used in place of a noun to avoid unnecessary repetition, e.g. I, we, she, they.

Proper noun   The label we give to a particular person, thing, place, or animal, e.g. Amundsen, Spain, Coca-Cola. Proper nouns always begin with a capital letter. See page 42.

Prose   Writing which is not poetry.

Punctuation   The marks we use in writing to make it easier to read and understand. See **Full stop**, **Question mark**, **Comma**, **Apostrophe**, and **Inverted commas**.

Purpose   The particular reason we have for writing or saying something, e.g. our purpose might be to persuade somebody, to give information, or to entertain them.

Question mark   The punctuation mark (?) used at the end of a sentence or a speech in dialogue to show that it is a question, e.g. Is that right? But what could we do? What do you want?

Quotation marks   See **Inverted commas**.

Received pronunciation   The 'neutral' or 'standard' accent that some people use instead of a regional accent. See also **Accent**.

Reported speech   The words that are spoken by a character in a story or a person in an article, but which are reported by the narrator or writer, rather than reproduced word-for-word. See pages 42, 155.

Rhyme   Words rhyme when their endings have the same sounds, e.g. *seeds, weeds*, or similar sounds, e.g. *name, again*.

Rhythm   The 'beat' of a poem. The rhythm might be fast, smooth, or irregular, for example. A limerick has a very noticeable rhythm.

Sentence   A group of words which makes sense. Sentences always begin with a capital letter and end with a full stop, question mark or exclamation mark. They usually contain a main verb. A **simple sentence** says just one thing, e.g. Caesar was powerful. When we join two sentences with 'or', 'and' or 'but' we make a **coordinated sentence**, e.g. The conspirators met *and* decided to kill him. When we use a different conjunction to show how the two parts of the sentence are connected in meaning, we make a **complex sentence**, e.g. The conspirators killed him *because* he had grown too powerful. See page 118.

Simile   A way of comparing things in an unusual or unexpected way, in which the writer uses the words 'like' or 'as', e.g. and catherine-wheels begin to flame *like* whirling marigolds.

Singular   See **Noun**.

Slang   A special form of language used by particular groups in informal situations, sometimes to add vividness or humour. See page 116.

Speech marks   See **Inverted commas**.

Stage directions   Information in a play text provided by the playwright to help the reader or actor understand what is happening, what the set looks like, or how a character says or does something. See page 154.

Standard English dialect   The dialect that is heard in all parts of the country and is understood throughout the English-speaking world. Nearly all writing is in Standard English dialect and it is the dialect of public communication.

Statement   See **Sentence**.

Synonym   A word which means the same, or almost the same, as another word, e.g. *happy, merry* and *cheerful*. See pages 78–79.

Tense   The form of the verb which tells us when something happens. Verbs can be in the **present tense**, e.g. This *is* one of Flint's jokes. Or the past tense, e.g. A skeleton *lay* on the sand. Or the **future tense**, e.g. We *will* sail on the next tide.

Topic   The subject of a piece of writing or speech. The topics of extracts in the Non-fiction module include Arriving in Spain, Coca-Cola, and Roald Amundsen.

Verb   The word in a sentence which enables us to say what people or things are *doing*, e.g. I *lay* down and *stretched* out full length … ; or *being*, e.g. The moon *was* full. Verbs can be in the **first person**, e.g. *I* (or *we*) went out; the **second person**, e.g. *You* left your coat behind; or in the **third person**, e.g. *She* (or *he, it* or *they*) came back. See pages 76–77; also **Tense**.

Word class   A group of words which do a particular job in a sentence, e.g. nouns label people, places, things, or ideas; pronouns take the place of nouns. They are sometimes called **Parts of speech**. The word classes referred to in this book are nouns (proper nouns, common nouns, abstract nouns, and collective nouns), adjectives, verbs, adverbs, conjunctions, and pronouns.

Index of Authors and Extracts

Note: page numbers in italics refer to where texts are used in Language Study.

Acknowledgements

We are grateful for permission to reproduce the following copyright material:

Module 1 – Narrative
Beverly Cleary: extracts from *Dear Mr Henshaw*, © 1983 Beverly Cleary, reprinted by permission of the publisher, Walker Books Limited, London. **Yvonne Coppard:** extract from *Not Dressed Like That, You Don't*, reprinted by permission of the publishers, Piccadilly Press Ltd. **Zlata Filipovic:** extracts from *Zlata's Diary* translated by Christina Pribichevich-Zori, Copyright © Fixot et editions Robert Laffont 1993 (Puffin Books 1995), reprinted by permission of the publishers. **Anne Fine:** abridged extract from *Goggle Eyes*, Copyright © Anne Fine 1989 (first published by Hamish Hamilton Children's Books, 1989), reprinted by permission of Penguin Books Ltd. **Adele Geras:** extract from 'The Dollmaker' © Adele Geras 1982 from *Letters of Fire* (Hamish Hamilton), reprinted by permission of Laura Cecil on behalf of the author. **Jill Paton Walsh:** extract from *Fireweed* (Viking Kestrel), reprinted by permission of David Higham Associates. **Gary Paulsen:** extract from *Nightjohn* (Macmillan Children's Books 1994), reprinted by permission of Macmillan Publishers. **Dylan Thomas:** extract from *Under Milk Wood* (J M Dent 1954), reprinted by permission of David Higham Associates. **Robert Westall:** extracts from 'The Call' in *The Call and Other Stories*, Copyright © Robert Westall 1989 (first published by Viking Children's Books, 1989), reprinted by permission of Penguin Books Ltd. **Chris Westwood:** extract from *A Light in the Black*, Copyright © Chris Westwood 1989 (first published by Viking Children's Books, 1989), reprinted by permission of Penguin Books Ltd.

Module 2 – Poetry
James Berry: 'Dog' and 'Broom' both from *When I Dance* by James Berry, Copyright © James Berry 1988 (first published by Hamish Hamilton Children's Books, 1988), reprinted by permission of Penguin Books Ltd. **Charles Causley:** 'Why' from *Collected Poems* (Macmillan 1987), reprinted by permission of David Higham Associates. **Carol Chopping:** limerick 'Dad waited...' found in E O Parrott (ed): *Limerick Delight* (Puffin), author not traced. **Gillian Clarke:** 'The Spider' and explanatory text from Helen Cook and Morag Styles (eds): *There's a Poet Behind You* (A & C Black 1988), reprinted by permission of A & C Black (Publishers) Ltd; 'My Box' and 'Nightride' from *Selected Poems* (Carcanet 1985), reprinted by permission of Carcanet Press Limited. **John Cotton:** Two riddles from *Two by Two* (with Fred Sedgwick) first published by Mary Glasgow Publications 1990, reprinted by permission of the author. **Sue Cowling:** 'Dustbin Liner' found in Gerard Benson (ed): *This Poem Doesn't Rhyme* (Puffin 1992). Copyright Sue Cowling, author not traced. **Kevin Crossley-Holland:** extract from *Beowulf* (OUP 1982), reprinted by permission of Oxford University Press. **Gina Douthwaite:** Five Haiku first published in John Foster (ed): *Let's Celebrate* (OUP 1989), reprinted by permission of the author. **Philip Gross:** extracts from 'Mirror, Mirror' from The All-Nite Cafe by Philip Gross, reprinted by permission of Faber & Faber Ltd. **John Manifold:** 'The Griesly Wife' from *Collected Verse* (University of Queensland Press, St Lucia, 1978), reprinted by permission of the publishers. **Trevor Millum:** 'Birthdays' from Ian McMillan (ed): *Against the Grain* (Nelson 1989) reprinted by permission of the author. **Adrian Mitchell:** 'Use your feet' and 'Maybe the search for food' from *The Thirteen Secrets of Poetry* (Simon & Schuster), reprinted by permission of the Peters Fraser & Dunlop Group Ltd. **John Mole:** 'Grand and solo' and 'I am the shame...' Copyright © John Mole 1987 from *Boo to a Goose* (Peterloo 1987), and 'I am an instrument...' Copyright © John Mole 1990 from *The Mad Parrot's Countdown* (Peterloo 1990), reprinted by permission of Peterloo Poets. **Grace Nichols:** 'For Forest' and 'Sun is Laughing', Copyright © Grace Nichols 1988, 1990, from John Agard (ed): *A Caribbean Dozen* (Walker Books), reprinted by permission of Curtis Brown Group Ltd, London on behalf of Grace Nichols. **Judith Nicholls:** 'Magic Mirror' and 'Teacher Said' from *Magic Mirror and Other Poems for Children* by Judith Nicholls, reprinted by permission of Faber & Faber Ltd. **Gareth Owen:** 'Growing Up' from *Song of the City* (1985), reprinted by permission of HarperCollins Publishers Ltd. **James Reeves:** 'Fireworks' from *The Blackbird in the Lilac*, © James Reeves from *Complete Poems for Children* (Heinemann), reprinted by permission of Laura Cecil on behalf of the James Reeves Estate. **Frank Richards:** Two limericks found in E O Parrott (ed): *Limerick Delight* (Penguin) reprinted by permission of the author. **Lemn Sissay:** 'Rhythm' first published in *Tender Fingers in a Clenched Fist* (Bogle L'Overture), reprinted by permission of the author. **Brian Stone:** No. 61 ['Swarthy smoke-blackened smiths, smudged with soot'] from *Medaeval English Verse* translated by Brian Stone (Penguin Classics, 1964), Copyright © Brian Stone 1964, reprinted by permission of Penguin Books Ltd. **Kit Wright:** 'The Magic Box' from *Cat Among the Pigeons* by Kit Wright, Copyright © Kit Wright 1984 (first published in Viking Children's Books, 1987), reprinted by permission of Penguin Books Ltd. **Benjamin Zephaniah:** 'Vegan Delight' from *Talking Turkeys* by Benjamin Zephaniah, Copyright © Benjamin Zephaniah 1994 (first published in Viking Children's Books, 1994), reprinted by permission of Penguin Books Ltd. Three traditional limericks from E O Parrott (ed): *Limerick Delight*, reprinted by permission of Penguin Books Ltd.

Module 3 – Non-Fiction
Brittany Ferries: for extract from 1995 'Gîte Holidays in France' brochure. **Coca-Cola Great Britain and Ireland:** for Coca-Cola logo, and extracts and illustrations from *The Chronicle of Coca-Cola*. **The Guardian:** for extract from article 'Real thing with Coke as Sales Top League', Copyright © The Guardian 1993. **HarperCollins Publishers Ltd:** for extract from *A Traveller's Life* by Eric Newby (Picador 1982). **Hodder Headline plc:** for extract from Patricia Marne: *Graphology* (Hodder & Stoughton, 1980). **Newspaper Publishing plc:** for extract from article 'Kobe Steeled for the Aftershock' by Peter McGill from *The Independent on Sunday*, 22.1.95. **Penguin Books Ltd:** for entries for 'Violence' (pp 70-71) and 'Burst' (p 484) from *Roget's Thesaurus of English Words and Phrases* edited by Susan M Lloyd (Penguin Books 1966, first published by Longman 1962), Copyright © Longman Green & Co. Ltd. 1962, 1966, 1982. **The Rank Organisation/Haven Leisure Limited:** for extract from 'Haven 1995' brochure. **D C Thomson & Co Ltd:** for extracts from *Shout* magazine, © D.C. Thomson & Co. Ltd 1994. **Thomson Tour Operations Limited:** for extracts from 'Thomson Summer Sun 1995' and 'Horizon Summer Selection, April-October 1995' brochures. **The Yorkshire Evening Press:** for extract from article 'Ex-York Vicar Survives Quake' from *The Yorkshire Evening Press*, 20.1.95. The following pupils from **Huntington School, York** for handwriting extracts: (A) Gemma Murray, (B) Judith Rankin, (C) Naazlin Karbani, (D) Talia Lyon, and (E) Christian Hasner-Myerscough.

Module 4 – Drama
The Bible: extracts from *New English Bible*, © Oxford University Press and Cambridge University Press 1961, 1970, reprinted by permission of Cambridge University Press. **Robert Bolt:** extract from *The Thwarting of Baron Bolligrew* (Heinemann, 1966) reprinted by permission of Heinemann Publishers (Oxford) Ltd. **Geoffrey Chaucer:** extracts from the Prologue to *The Canterbury Tales*, from *The Riverside Chaucer*, edited by Larry D Benson, Copyright © 1987 by Houghton Mifflin Company, reprinted by permission of the publisher. **Richard Curtis and Ben Elton:** transcript extract from BBC Television series *Blackadder Goes Forth*, 'Captain Cook', reprinted by permission of the Peters Fraser and Dunlop Group Ltd. **Rob Grant and Doug Naylor:** transcript extract from *Red Dwarf* series 3 'Polymorph', © Rob Grant and Doug Naylor 1989 (stage directions not original –